THE PROVERB

LONDON : HUMPHREY MILFORD

OXFORD UNIVERSITY PRESS

THE PROVERB

BY

ARCHER TAYLOR

HARVARD · UNIVERSITY · PRESS

CAMBRIDGE · MASSACHUSETTS

1931

PRINTED AT THE HARVARD UNIVERSITY PRESS

CAMBRIDGE, MASS., U.S.A.

To

MY MOTHER

PREFACE

THE proverb and related forms have long been objects of general interest and the occasion for many books, but they have attracted little serious and thorough study. As a result, fundamental problems are neglected and even their existence is not clearly realized. After all, we know little or nothing of the origin, dissemination, and literary style of proverbs. Books give us curious and often unreliable information on these matters, although rarely systematically or in such a fashion as to permit or encourage the reader to look farther. Proverbs attract people interested in the didactic or in the quaint and strange, and neither group is noted for thoroughness or accuracy. To be sure, diligent scholars have spent lifetimes of labor in making storehouses of materials for the use of future generations, but as yet this wealth has profited us little. Its utilization requires constant attention to detail and a clear perception of aims and methods.

In the following pages I have endeavored to describe briefly and systematically the ways in which proverbs arise, the kinds of proverbs, and the details of proverbial style. It has seemed inadvisable to seek examples outside the ordinary European languages, where we have a fairly distinct cultural tradition and clearly marked proverbial types. What is true of the English proverb is, in the main, true of the German or the French proverb. Oriental, African, Malay,

Japanese, or Chinese proverbs involve such widely differing cultural spheres and have in general so little connection with European proverbs that I have not hesitated to leave them out.

For the scholar's convenience I have compiled an index of the English, German, and Latin proverbs cited, and in it I have given what seemed to me the most useful references from works on the comparative study of proverbs. So far as possible, I have listed all proverbs under English forms with cross-references from German and Latin. For proverbs from other languages, when no parallel English, German, or Latin form appears in this book, I give sources and references in foot-notes. Proverbs which do not appear in the index and which are not supported by a reference are cited from oral tradition. I have profited by the opportunity offered by the index to cite additional proverbs and the literature on them. Such additional proverbs set interesting and important problems for future study, problems which I have discussed at sufficient length and which do not call for further illustration. This index will appear in *FF Communications* (Helsinki).

Suggestions and encouragement from Margaret Hardie and Richard Jente, who read this book in manuscript, have added to its usefulness and value. The scholarship of my teacher, George Lyman Kittredge, has enriched this book as it has enriched and enlarged my life and ideals.

CHICAGO, June 8, 1931.

CONTENTS

THE PROVERB

I

THE ORIGINS OF THE PROVERB

THE definition of a proverb is too difficult to repay the undertaking; and should we fortunately combine in a single definition all the essential elements and give each the proper emphasis, we should not even then have a touchstone. An incommunicable quality tells us this sentence is proverbial and that one is not. Hence no definition will enable us to identify positively a sentence as proverbial. Those who do not speak a language can never recognize all its proverbs, and similarly much that is truly proverbial escapes us in Elizabethan and older English. Let us be content with recognizing that a proverb is a saying current among the folk. At least so much of a definition is indisputable, and we shall see and weigh the significance of other elements later.

The origins of the proverb have been little studied. We can only rarely see a proverb actually in the making, and any beliefs we have regarding origins must justify themselves as evident or at least plausible. Proverbs are invented in several ways: some are simple apothegms and platitudes elevated to proverbial dignity, others arise from the symbolic or metaphoric use of an incident, still others imitate already existing proverbs, and some owe their existence to the condensing of a story or fable. It is convenient to distinguish as "learned" proverbs those with a long literary history. This literary history may begin in some apt Biblical or classical phrase, or it may go back to a more recent source. Such "learned" proverbs differ, however, in only this regard from other proverbs. Whatever the later history may be, the manner of ultimate invention of all proverbs, "learned" or "popular," falls under one or another of the preceding heads.

It is not proper to make any distinction in the treatment of "learned" and "popular" proverbs. The same problems exist for all proverbs with the obvious limitation that, in certain cases, historical studies are greatly restricted by the accidents of preservation. We can ordinarily trace the "learned" proverb down a long line of literary tradition, from the classics or the Bible through the Middle Ages to the present, while we may not be so fortunate with every "popular" proverb. For example, *Know thyself* may very well have been a proverb long before it was attributed to any of the seven wise men or was inscribed on the walls of the temple of Delphic Apollo. Juvenal was nearer the truth when he said it came from Heaven: "E caelo descendit γνῶθι σεαυτόν" (*Sat.*, xi, 27). Yet so far as modern life is concerned, the phrase owes its vitality to centuries of bookish tradition. St. Jerome termed *Don't look a gift horse in the mouth* a common proverb, when he used it to refer to certain writings which he had regarded as free-will offerings and which critics had found fault with: "Noli (ut vulgare est proverbium) equi dentes inspicere donati." We cannot hope to discover whether the modern proverb owes its vitality to St. Jerome or to the vernacular tradition on which he was drawing. St. Jerome also took *The wearer best knows where the shoe wrings him* from Plutarch, but we may conjecture that this proverb, too, was first current on the lips of the folk. Obviously the distinction between "learned" and "popular" is meaningless and is concerned merely with the accidents of history.

Proverbial Apothegms

Often some simple apothegm is repeated so many times that it gains proverbial currency: *Live and learn*; *Mistakes will happen*; *Them as has gets*; *Enough is enough*; *No fool like an old fool*; *Haste makes waste*; *Business is business*; *What's done's done*. Characteristic of such proverbs is the absence of metaphor. They consist merely of a bald assertion which is recognized as proverbial only because we have heard it often and because it can be applied to many different situations. It is ordinarily difficult, if not impossible, to determine the age of such proverbial truisms. The simple truths of life have been noted in every age, and it must not surprise us that one such truth has a long recorded history while another has none. It is only chance, for example, that *There is a time for every-thing* has a long history in English, — Shakespere used it in the *Comedy of Errors*, ii, 2: "There's a time for all things," — and it is even in the Bible: "To every thing there is a season, and a time to every pur-pose under the heaven" (Omnia tempus habent, et suis spatiis transeunt universa sub caelo, *Eccles.* iii, 1), while *Mistakes will happen* or *If you want a thing well done, do it yourself* have, on the contrary, no his-tory at all.

Just such proverbs as these simple apothegms are perhaps the most difficult of all to recognize in a later age when they have ceased to circulate and when our ears are deaf to their value as oft-repeated sayings. We shall never know, for example, which of the Ex-eter Gnomes in Old English poetry are proverbial and which are the collector's moralizing in the same pattern. In the ears of the Anglo-Saxon author there may have been a proverbial ring to such truisms as

The frost shall freeze, fire consume wood, the earth sprout, ice shall form a bridge. . . . The sea shall be rest-less. The solemn way of the dead is longest secret. Holly shall go to the fire. The property of a dead man shall be divided. Fame is best.

Even so, the possibility of demonstrating proverbial usage in such cases hardly exists in the scanty poetic remains at our disposal. In a dead language the means which are available are various, but not al-ways effective or easily applied. A passage, when it

varies grammatically or syntactically from ordinary
usage or from the usage of the context, can be safely
declared to be proverbial. The test of proverbial
style may be invoked: *At home everything is easy*
(Dælt er heima hvat)[1] has the terseness of a proverb
and so has *Better blind than burned*, i. e. 'dead' (Blindr
er betri, en brendr sé).[2] In an alliterative poem, that
is to say, in almost all old Germanic poetry, a defect
in the alliteration warns us that the poet was using
materials which he could not rephrase to suit his immediate metrical needs and calls our attention to the
presence of a proverb, e. g. *Bú er betra, þótt lítit sé*
('[One's own] home is better, though it be small').[3]
Here we observe that alliteration is absent in the second half-line, although it is demanded by the rules
of Old Norse versification. The most convincing evidence is, of course, the actual proverbial use elsewhere
of the doubtful passage, and, above all, its use in con-
texts where it cannot easily be a quotation from the
passage under examination. The Icelandic *Two are
an army against one* (Tveir ro eins heriar) is clearly a
proverb, for we have the same phrase in Middle High
German (Zwêne sint eines her, *Iwein*, l. 5350) and in
mediaeval Latin (Duo sunt exercitus uni, *Ysengrimus*,
ii, 311). Two Old High German expressions *When it
rains, the trees become wet* (So iz regenôt, sô nazscênt tê

1 Heusler, *Zeitschrift des Vereins für Volkskunde*, XXV (1915), 110,
 No. 1.
2 The same, 113, No. 27.
3 The same, 111, No. 4.

bouma) and *When it blows, the trees shake* (So iz uuât, sô uuagônt tê bouma) are certainly proverbs, for the first is found again in a manuscript collection of the fourteenth century, and the second is in a modern collection of Low German proverbs. In such instances as these last proverbs the metaphorical application of the situation has lost all meaning for us.

Proverbs originating in apothegms contain a moral or ethical truth, although often in a form which utterly lacks dignity, e. g. *One should keep old roads and old friends* (Alt weg und alt freundt soll man behalten). *God is above all* (God es boven al) is a proverb frequently used in Elizabethan England, and before that in Holland; but it seems to us no more than a platitude. Such wholly commonplace phrases are still found in proverbial use: *A place for everything and everything in its place*; *You never can tell till you've tried*; *A man can die but once*; *All men must die*; *Seeing is believing*; *If you want a thing well done, do it yourself*.

Such truisms and platitudes gain proverbial significance from implication and use, that is, from vague emotional and connotational values which can mean little to another age and give these homely sentences a meaning beyond the simple and obvious uses of the words involved. A similar change has occurred in every proverb, and ordinarily takes the form of a metaphor; but in these simple platitudes the change does not attain metaphorical dignity.

Simple maxims find a ready response in naïve minds. Such admonitions as *Everything comes to him who waits*; *Steady and slow go far in a day*; *Set a thief to catch a thief*; *If you can't be good, be careful*;[1] *A young man married is a young man marred* have provided many with standards of conduct and guiding principles for life. The stock broker couches warning counsel in similar terms: *Cut your losses and let your profits run*; *You never lost money taking a profit*; *Don't sell America short*. Some maxims have only a brief life. *Let George do it*, which is perhaps a vaudeville phrase, is now less frequently heard than formerly and is perhaps on its way to extinction.[2]

In some maxims the age or the circumstances of origin are more or less distinctly suggested, but ordinarily we cannot even guess when or how they came into being. *Money talks* may be a saying of the stock market or the poker game.[3] *Dead men tell no tales* arose in a ruthless, quarrelsome society. Although we are perhaps inclined to associate it with the moral code of a pirate, it must be older than Captain Kidd and belong to a somewhat higher social level, for it is already an established proverb in Elizabethan times. *The*

1 An old maxim. Compare *Caute, si non caste.* In France, our soldiers paraphrased it as *If you can't be good, be sanitary.*

2 Possibly we can see a connection with *Laissez faire à George, il est homme d'âge*, a historical proverb. We are told that Louis XII expressed his confidence in his minister, George d'Amboise, in these words. The traditional explanation in America is based on "George" as a name used in addressing Pullman porters.

3 Cf. "Argens fait le jeu" (*Baudoin de Sebourc*, xxiv, 443).

only good Indian is a dead Indian breathes the air of our own western frontier. The warning *Watch your step* employs a metaphor from the New York subway or the Pullman sleeping car.

METAPHORICAL PROVERBS

The most interesting and artistic proverbs arise from the metaphorical use of a simple act or event: *Fish or cut bait*; *Chickens come home to roost*; *Vinegar catches no flies*; *Soft fire makes sweet malt*; *Barking dogs never bite*; *You can lead a horse to water, but you can't make him drink*. A novel application of a familiar scene arrests our attention, imprints itself on our minds, and drives home the lesson. Of all the ways in which proverbs develop, the most important is illustrated by such extensions of the meaning of a simple phrase. By this process a sentence comes to mean far more than the sum of the words composing it. *New brooms sweep clean* is a housewife's observation of fact, but as a proverb it may find use in any field. An important corollary to this is the fact that no single application of a proverb exhausts its meaning. Except in a vague paraphrase there is no defining a proverb.

Some metaphorical proverbs are as old as any that we know. Others have no history: they appear for the first time in recent collections or are perhaps even yet unrecorded. The temptation to reprint older sources without real effort to enlarge them or to verify them by reference to oral tradition, a temptation which besets all collectors, makes even the best modern collections unreliable guides to the stock of current proverbs. In English the situation is particularly serious: hardly any of the available collections is entirely trustworthy.

Dateless as such recent or unrecorded proverbs necessarily are, they are nevertheless of great interest. As we shall see later, internal evidence or comparison with proverbs in other languages often gives us a hint of their age and history. A few instances will show how erroneous is Tylor's notion [1] that the age of proverb-making is past. "We can collect and use the old proverbs," he says, "but making new ones has become a feeble, spiritless imitation, like our attempts to invent new myths or new nursery rhymes." Certainly *Put up or shut up!* possesses as much vitality as can be demanded of a proverb, and from the metaphor we can safely conclude that it is not many generations old. *No tickee, no washee*, i. e. 'without the essential prerequisite, a desired object cannot be obtained,' with its evident allusion to the Chinese laundryman, bespeaks for itself a still more recent origin. *Three generations from shirtsleeves to shirtsleeves* is an invention of yesterday, but there are English parallels, e. g. *There is nobbut three generations atween clogs and clogs*, which carry its ultimate beginnings back to England. For the origin of such proverbs as *Every*

[1] *Primitive Culture*, I, ch. iii, 89–90.

man must skin his own skunk; *It pays to advertise*; *Paddle your own canoe*; *Read 'em and weep*; *Don't take any wooden nickels*; *One boy's a boy, two boys is half a boy, three boys is no boy at all*, we need not look outside of America. It would be more correct to say that proverb-making, as well as the interest in proverbs, exhibits remarkable fluctuations from age to age. To this subject we must return later.

Proverbs which smack of the soil and the folk, and yet have no long history so far as our records go, exist in great numbers. The naïve metaphor involved in them has struck popular fancy, and the proverb lingers in tradition. Examples of such proverbs are: *A short horse is soon curried*; *A shady lane breeds mud,* i. e. 'secrecy creates wrong-doing or scandal'; *You never miss a slice from a cut loaf*; *Politics makes strange bedfellows*; *Don't bite the hand that feeds you*; *Money makes the mare go*; *The grey mare is the better horse*, i. e. 'the wife is more competent than the husband,' which is as old as 1546; *Don't bite off more than you can chew*; *Don't cut off your nose to spite your face*; *You can't get blood out of a turnip*; *Dog eat dog*; *You can't spoil a rotten egg.*

Naturally such tradition draws its materials from the interests and the world of the common man. There is little or no question here of "gesunkenes Kulturgut," intellectual materials which were shaped in higher social circles and have descended from them to lower ones. Possibly the very fashion of proverbs as a manner of expression has descended in this way; but certainly most proverbs actually current in oral tradition have been coined by the folk, whatever the ultimate models may have been. The metaphors are chosen from the household and the simple events of life: *A burnt child dreads the fire*; *You must learn to creep before you can go* (i. e. 'walk'); *There's many a slip between cup and lip*; *When the cat's away, the mice will play*; *Half a loaf is better than no bread*; *The pot calls the kettle black*; *Every tub must stand on its own bottom*; *The proof of the pudding is in the eating*; *An ill weed spoils a whole pot of pottage*; *A drowning man will catch at a straw*; *There is no smoke without fire*; *It's ill halting before a cripple*. The peasant's world, the farmstead and the countryside, yields many an observation which lends itself to metaphorical use in a proverb: *Don't count your chickens before they are hatched*; *A ragged colt may make a good horse*; *A cock is mighty on his own dunghill*; *Curst cows have short horns*; *A cur will bite before he will bark*; *Make hay while the sun shines*; *Look before you leap*; *It's a long road that has no turning*; *Steady and slow go far in a day*; *The master's eye makes the horse fat*; *The still sow eats up all the draff*.

As we might expect, hunting and fishing provide us with a goodly share of proverbs: *All fish are not caught with flies*; *It is good fishing in troubled waters*; *It is ill fishing before the net*; *A bird in the hand is worth two in the bush*; *A miss is as good as a mile*. So far as my ob-

servation goes, proverbs alluding to fishing are somewhat more numerous than those alluding to hunting.[1]

Proverbs which show themselves to be the invention of sailors are not abundant.[2] *A stern chase is a
long chase* is a familiar saying, and a few others might
be collected; but Apperson's large dictionary of English proverbs does not include many sea proverbs.

Proverbs which clearly reflect village life, e.g. *Sweep
in front of your own door*, or which imply any form
of society more highly organized than the single
household complete within itself, are comparatively
rare. Such sayings as *A stitch in time saves nine* or
The shoe will hold with the sole need have of course no

1 See the bibliography in Bonser, *Proverb Literature* (London, 1930),
  p. 434, Nos. 3791–3797.
2 Sea proverbs have been collected for their own sake. Perhaps the first
  work which makes special mention of such proverbs is a Dutch dictionary of sea terms (W. A. Winschoten, *Seeman* [Leiden, 1681]).
  F. A. Stoett extracts some curious superstitions and words from this
  work; see "W. A. Winschoten's Seeman," *De Nieuwe Taalgids*, XIII
  (1919), 97–106. For Dutch sea proverbs see van Dam van Isselt,
  Nederlandsche Muzen-Almanak (1838), pp. 135–139, and particularly
  Sprenger van Eijk (*Handleiding tot de Kennis van onze Vaderlandsche
  Spreekwoorden . . . van de Scheepvaart en het Scheepsleven Ontleend*
  [Rotterdam 1835–36]). D. H. van der Meer (*Verzameling van Stukken
  betreffende de Friesche Geschiedenis*, etc. [Franeker, n.d.], I, 121–133)
  notes some Frisian sea proverbs. Sébillot (*Légendes, Croyances, et
  Superstitions de la Mer* [Paris, 1886–87]) and Corbière ("Des Proverbes
  Nautiques," *Revue de Rouen et de la Normandie*, Vol. XIII [1845])
  collect French examples. English and German collections have been
  made by Cowan (*A Dictionary of the Proverbs and Proverbial Expressions Relating to the Sea* [Greenesburgh, Pennsylvania, 1894]), Lypkes
  (*Seemannssprüche* [Berlin, 1900]), and in the anonymous *Sea Words
  and Phrases along the Suffolk Coast* (Lowestoft, 1869–70), a reprinting
  of articles from the *East Anglian Notes and Queries*, January, 1869 and
  January, 1870.

larger background than the household, while on the other hand *The cobbler's wife is always ill shod* and *Cobbler, stick to your last!* are metaphors based on a trade. In general, proverbs reflect the peasant's or common man's attitude toward a particular calling: the miller and the tailor are objects of suspicion. If we disregard proverbs of this class, to which such a book as Rudolf Eckart's *Stand und Beruf im Volksmunde* (1900) is primarily devoted, we shall have very few left.

The trades and mercantile pursuits have coined almost no proverbs.[1] *A cunning knave needs no broker* is a peasant's observation of the course of the world and involves some notion of its organization, but the proverb is not the invention of a broker. A few sayings from the stock market have been accepted as proverbial. Such a book as F. López Toral's *El Evangelio de los Comerciantes ó Explicación de los Refranes ... para Todos se dedican á la Práctica del Comercio* (The Merchant's Bible or the Interpretation of Proverbs ... for All who occupy Themselves with Business),[2] which I have been unable to obtain, would be very interesting. The clerk, the miner, the mason, the butcher, the printer, the painter, the smith (*Strike while the iron is hot*), the weaver, the carpenter (*A carpenter is known by his chips*), and the merchant are almost silent in the world of proverbs.

1 See the bibliography in Bonser, *Proverb Literature* (London, 1930), pp. 447–448, Nos. 3914–3927.
2 Zaragoza, 1899.

Proverbial Types

New proverbs have often been made on old models. Certain frames lend themselves readily to the insertion of entirely new ideas. Thus the contrast in *Young . . ., old . . .* in such a proverb as *Young saint, old devil* yields a model for *Junge Bettschwester, alte Betschwester*. A methodical comparison would probably reveal the proverb which gave the original impulse to the formation of the others; but no one has ever undertaken a study of this sort. Martha Lenschau conceives the development as follows: *Young angel, old devil* (Jung Engel, alt Teufel, thirteenth century); *Young knights, old beggars* (Junge Ritter, alte Bettler, sixteenth century); *Young soldiers, old beggars* (Junge Soldaten, alte Bettler, seventeenth century). The first form made no distinction for sex. When the substitution of "knight" or "soldier" made the distinction, a by-form for women was invented on the same model: *Junge Hure, alt Kupplerin* appears to have been the first of such by-forms, although *Jung Hure, alt Wettermacherin* must also be ancient, since the notion involved in "Wettermacherin" reaches far back. The most recent development is probably the Low German *Young gamblers, old beggars* (Junge Späler, ole Bedler), and the corruption *Young musicians, old beggars* (Junge Musikanten, alde Beddellüde), which arises from the misunderstanding of "Späler," 'players' (i. e. gamblers), as 'players of music' and the later substitution of a synonym.

It is not always easy to recognize or identify the earliest form which provided the model for later developments; and until several proverbs have been minutely examined from this point of view and our methods of study have been improved, it is hard to say which arguments are safe to use and which are unsafe. In all probability, we may trust to the general principles which have been worked out for märchen, i. e. those employed in the so-called Finnish or historico-geographical method. The relative age and distribution of the various forms of a proverb will throw much light on the development. In the present instance, for example, we might regard the old and widely known *Jung gewohnt, alt getan* ('What one is accustomed to in youth, one does in old age') as a possible model, even of the whole group. Certainly it has given us *Jung gefreut, alt gereut* ('Rejoiced in youth, repented in age') and as a secondary development: *Jung gefreit, alt gereut* ('Married in youth, repented in age'). Since, however, *Young saint, old devil* is even older and more widely known, I am inclined to consider it the parent of all later forms. Often other arguments than age and wide currency may be brought into court. Usually, a dialectal variation which is essential to a particular form and which limits it to a narrow area is secondary in origin, e. g. *Jung gefreit, alt geklait* ('Wed in youth, bewailed

in old age') can have arisen only in a region where
"geklagt" is pronounced "geklait." So, too, *Jung
gefreit, alt gereut* originated in a region — somewhat
larger, to be sure, than the one just mentioned —
where the dialectal pronounciation of "gereut" made
the rhyme tolerable.

A few more illustrations of the creation of new
proverbs on the model of old ones will suffice. A familiar German proverbial type employs the notion that
the essential qualities of an object show themselves
from the very beginning, e. g. *Was ein Häkchen werden
soll, krümmt sich beizeiten* ('Whatever is to be a hook,
bends early'). English representatives of this type are
rare, but we may cite *Timely crooks that tree that will
be a cammock* (i. e. 'gambrel,' a bent piece of wood
used by butchers to hang carcasses on) and *It pricketh
betimes that shall be a sharp thorn*. A German derivative of the type is *Was ein Nessel werden soll, brennt
beizeiten* ('Whatever is to be a nettle, burns early').
This proverb has found rather wide currency. Although the evidence is not all in, the type or at least
its ready employment in new proverbs is German.
The form characteristic of *Es sind nicht alle Jäger,
die das Horn blasen* ('They are not all hunters who
blow horns'), a form which appears to have been first
recorded by Varro ('Non omnes, qui habent citharam,
sunt citharoedi'), enjoyed a remarkable popularity
in mediaeval Germany and gave rise to many new
proverbs, e. g. *They are not all cooks who carry long*

knives (Es sind nicht alle Köche, die lange Messer tragen); *They are not all friends who laugh with you* (Zijn niet alle vrienden, die hem toelachen). Outside of Germany and countries allied culturally, the form appears to have had no notable success, except in *All is not gold that glitters*, which refers to a thing and not a person. Seiler thinks that "Many are called, but few are chosen" (Multi enim sunt vocati, pauci vero electi, *Matt.* xx, 16; xxii, 14) was the ultimate model for these proverbs, but the similarity is one of thought and not of form. Possibly one could imagine a class based on simple balance and contrast, of which the *young-old* type and the *called-chosen* type might both be derivatives, but the fundamental differences in syntactical structure speak strongly against a development of this sort. *Young saint, old devil* is an old proverbial form which has no verb; *Many are called, but few are chosen* consists of balanced, antithetical sentences; *All is not gold that glitters* uses a subordinate clause. The syntactical differences are so great that an influence from one of these types on another does not seem likely.

Not all proverbial types have been equally successful in propagating themselves. *One swallow does not make a summer* gives us *One man does not make a dance* (Unus homo non facit choream) and *One man does not make a team*, but it has not been very productive otherwise. *After the calm comes a storm* appears to have preceded *After joy comes annoy*; and *Quem ode-*

rint dii, hunc pedagogem fecerunt ('Whom the gods
hate, they make a teacher') is a derivative of the
anonymous *Quem Deus perdere vult, dementat prius*
('Whom God wishes to destroy, he first drives mad'),
a Christian version of *Quem Iuppiter perdere vult,
dementat prius* (a maxim of obscure origin which may
have been invented in Cambridge about 1640) and of
such other phrases as the Plautine and Menandrian
"Whom the Gods love, die young" (Quem di diligunt
Adulescens moritur, *Bacch.*, ll. 816–817). *The tree falls
not at the first blow* (Der Baum fällt nicht vom ersten
Streiche) gave some butcher a model for *The ox does
not fall at the first blow* (Der Ochse fällt nicht vom
ersten Streiche). *Politics makes strange bedfellows* is
evidently a derivative of *Misery acquaints a man with
strange bedfellows* and *Poverty makes strange bedfellows*.
Such recently invented proverbs as *Politics makes
strange bedfellows* and *One man does not make a team*
show that new formations on old models are still possible in tradition; but forces which are not easy to
name or estimate determine whether a proverbial
type becomes widely creative. Clearly the first and
most important requirement is familiarity with the
formula. A single proverb is often widely enough
known to supply a model for many nonce-formations.
A second requirement is the applicability of the formula. Not all formulae can give rise to new proverbs.

Occasionally the history of a proverbial type is difficult to decipher. The saying *The nearer the church,*

the farther from God is old and widely known: the
English tradition, which is often scanty, dates from
1300 and the proverb is also found in German, Dutch,
Swedish (Finland), French, Italian, and no doubt other
languages. In the more easterly portions of Europe
(Bohemia, Poland, Hungary, Croatia; but also Denmark) a similar proverb declares *The nearer to church,
the later in* (Jo nærmere kirken, jo senere dertil). Another related form is *The nearer Rome, the worse Christian* (Quo Romae propiores, tanto christiani tepidi-
ores), which is first found in the early years of the
sixteenth century in Germany and countries culturally allied to Germany, and although it breathes the
hostile spirit of the German Reformation, a still more
violent and personal expression of the same mood is
found a generation earlier: *The nearer the Pope, the
worse Christian* (Zo nader den paeus, so quader ker-
sten). The eleventh-century *Fecunda Ratis* of Egbert
of Liège has "The nearer the fire, the hotter" (Tanto
plus calidum, quanto vicinius igni) and Chaucer says
"The ner the fire, the hatter is" (*Troilus*, i, 449).
Perhaps the latest invention on this model, although
it goes back to 1559 and, in Dutch, to an even earlier
time, is *The nearer the bone, the sweeter the meat*.
Clearly we have a single type according to which all
these proverbs have been made; but the age and distribution of the different forms do not seem to offer
much assistance in arriving at the archetype. The
proverbs involving Rome and the Pope we may dis-

card as later inventions, since neither their age nor their restriction to Germanic territory marks them as suitable models for later development. In this case we have almost at the very beginning of our history of the type a sharp division into certain clearly marked forms which show no obvious interrelations. To be sure, these difficulties may be more apparent than real; a minute examination might after all disclose new clues.

VARIATIONS OF PROVERBS IN TRADITION

Oral transmission creates minor variations in proverbs. These variations are produced by changes of the same general kinds as we find in märchen, ballads, and other popular materials: one specific detail is replaced by another; a general trait is replaced by a specific one, and vice versa; details suggested by similarity or contrast enter the proverb; expansions are brought about by the addition of duplicate or parallel traits; obsolete or misunderstood details are removed, and so on. The familiar proverb *A bird in the hand is worth two in the bush* illustrates many of the changes produced by oral transmission. The characteristic changes in the following examples concern first, the number of birds referred to; second, the place where the birds are seen; third, the kind of bird described. In 1562 John Heywood included *A birde in the hand is worth ten in the wood* in his epigrams, and still older is the form *A birde in hond is better than thre in the wode.* The Roumanians say *Better a bird in the hand than a thousand on the house*; the Italians, *Better one bird in the cage than four in the arbor*; and the Frisians, *A bird in the pan is better than many in the air.* The Latin forms *Una avis in laqueo plus valet octo vagis* ('A bird in the snare is worth more than eight flying'); *Plus valet in dextra passer, quam quatuor extra* ('One sparrow in the right hand is worth more than four out of it'); *Plus valet in manibus passer, quam sub dubio grus* ('A sparrow in the hands is worth more than a crane in doubt') have no parallels in the texts at hand. In such forms as these we have chiefly variations in number, although the reader will have already noticed some other incidental variations. A variation in regard to the location of either member of the comparison is very frequent: *Better a sparrow in the hand than two flying* (Portuguese); *Better one bird in the pot than ten in the wood* (Swedes in Finland); *Better a bird in the fist than ten in the wood* (Swedes in Finland); and *Better one bird in the cage than seven in the bush* (Swedes in Finland). We have already noted in the preceding examples the variation which replaces the general term "bird" by "sparrow." The simplest form of such characterization is *Better a little bird in the hand than a big bird in the wood* (Swedes in Finland). More interesting are the variations which deal with the species of the birds: *Better a sparrow in the hand than a crane on the roof* (German); *A sparrow in the hand is worth a vulture flying* (Spanish); *A finch in*

the hand is better than a thrush afar off (North Italian);
Better a bird in the hand than ten doves on the roof (Low
German); *Better a hawk in the hand than two in flight*
(Icelandic). The extent to which such alterations
can go is seen in the North Italian variants: *Better a
feather in the hand than a bird in the air*; *Better a sparrow in the pan than a hundred chickens in the pastor's
yard*; or the Finnish *Better a wood-grouse in the fist
than nine or two on the branch.*

A specific detail is replaced by a general one or vice
versa: *Where the Devil can't go, he sends an old woman*
(Wo der Teufel nicht hinkommen kann, schickt er ein
altes Weib), and the variant *Where the Devil can't go,
he sends his grandmother.* In the old proverb *The pot
goes so often to the well that it comes home broken* the
place is often named as "water" or "stream." Occasionally a reason can be found for the change. Thus
the old rhyme which the followers of John Ball sang
in 1381:

> When Adam delved and Eve span,
> Where was then the gentleman?

sets in parallel the words "delved" and "span,"
which belong to entirely different spheres of activity.
The Swedes in Finland have simplified the proverb by
referring to a single activity:

> Då Adam vävde och Eva spann,
> Var fanns då en adelsman?
> ('When Adam wove and Eve span,
> Where was there then the nobleman?')

The change was made easier by the similarity of "grävde" ('delved') and "vävde" ('wove'). In the variants of *Rome was not built in a day* the replacement of "Rome" by the names of other cities occurs frequently. Along the lower Rhine and westward we find Cologne and Aix-la-Chapelle, occasionally both together, in this proverb. In Brabant and Limburg they are replaced by Ghent and Bruges, e. g. *Gent en Brugge zijn op eenen dag niet gebouwd*, or Brussels and Ghent. The French name either Paris or Rome. Such substitutions are efforts to bring the proverb up to date or to accommodate it to a new country.

Another class of substitutions appears in the replacement of an object by its opposite; e. g. *A hasty bitch bears blind puppies* (Cagna frettolosa fa catellini ciechi) circulates in Italy also in the form *A hasty cat bears immature kittens* (Gatta frettolosa fa i gattini acerbi). It is not easy to find a general head under which to put such substitutions as *Much noise and little milk* (Viel Geschrei und wenig Milch) and *Much noise and few eggs* (Viel Geschrei und wenig Ei), which have developed from *Much noise and little wool* (Viel Geschrei und wenig Wolle).

A very characteristic way of making new forms consists in expansion by introducing new parallel or contrasting elements. Pope's verse "To err is human, to forgive, divine" (*Essay on Criticism*, l. 525), which has almost, if not entirely, established itself as a proverb, arises from *Errare est humanum* by employing the

logical contrast of "human" and "divine." The second part of *Pride goes before and shame comes after* has
developed in the same way. *Each man for himself*
seems to have been the first form, to which is later
added *and God for us all* or *and the Devil for all.* Now
the proverb runs *Every man for himself and the Devil
take the hindmost.* At the present moment the fact
that *Each man for himself and the Devil for all* is found
only in Florio's *First Fruits* (1578) does not concern
us. It is sufficient to note that we have two forms of
the proverb, one with "God" and one with "Devil."
We need not now inquire which came first, but it is
obvious that one produced the other by contrast.

Often the expansion is quite whimsical. Some wit,
I conjecture, has enlarged *I have other fish to fry* into
I have other fish to fry and their tails to butter. So, too,
arose *Neither fish, flesh, nor good red herring.* The old
proverb *Praise the fair day at even* has suffered many
an expansion of this sort, e. g. *Vespere laudatur lux,
hospes mane probatur* ('The day is praised in the evening, the host in the morning'); *Schöne Tage soll man
abends loben, schöne Frauen morgens* ('One should
praise beautiful days in the evening, beautiful women
in the morning'). So also *Clothes make the man* becomes
in German *Kleider machen Leute und Lumpen machen
Leuss* ('Clothes make the man and rags make lice'), a
form which apparently enjoyed some currency in the
sixteenth century. More casual modifications are
Clothes make people, priests make brides (Kleider

THE ORIGINS OF THE PROVERB 27

machen Leute, Pfaffen machen Bräute) and *Clothes make people, shoes the soldier* (Kleider machen Leute, Schuhe den Soldaten). In Essex they say *Every dog has his day, and a cat has two Sundays*. The addition *and a pudding has two* frequently occurs with the proverb *All things have an end*.

Proverbs Based on Narratives

In addition to making proverbs from other proverbs, tradition creates them from materials which seem at first sight more refractory. The relation of the fable and the proverb is particularly close, and not all nations have regarded them as distinct forms: the Greek αἶνος means both 'fable' and 'proverb.' So also the Aramaic-Syriac *mathla* and the related Hebrew *maschal* as well as the Old English *gied*. We are not well informed about the process of making fables into proverbs.[1] In general, it seems to be a characteristic of Oriental and savage proverbs. Many sayings of African and Asiatic peoples are entirely

1 See Otto, *Die Sprichwörter und Sprichwörtlichen Redensarten der Römer* (Leipzig, 1890), p. xxv; Bolte and Polívka, *Anmerkungun zu den Kinder- und Hausmärchen*, IV (1930), 116 n. 11, 365; "Fabel" in Pauly-Wissowa, *Realencyclopädie*; Crusius, "Märchenreminszenzen im Antiken Sprichwort," *Verhandlungen d. 40. Philologenversammlung zu Görlitz* (1890); L. Friedländer, *Bilder aus der Römischen Sittengeschichte*, I (5th ed., 1881), 469 ff., I (6th ed., 1888), 522 ff.; Büchmann, *Geflügelte Worte* (Berlin, 1920), pp. 71–86; Seiler, *Lehnsprichwort*, I, 22 f., 83 f.; Jente, "Märchen im Sprichwort," *Handbuch des Deutschen Märchens* (forthcoming). The article by Kasumović (*Rad* of the Jugoslav Academy, CXCI, 195), which is cited in *Zeitschrift des Vereins für Volkskunde*, XXIII (1913), 317, has not been accessible to me.

unintelligible to us because we do not know the story
behind the allusion. There may perhaps be certain
classes of stories which yield proverbs more readily
than others. The Aesopic fable, for example, stands
godfather to many a proverb: *Sour grapes*; *A dog in
the manger*; *Don't kill the goose that lays the golden
eggs*; *Don't count your chickens before they are hatched*
(which belongs in the modern Aesopic tradition, although it is not part of the original stock of fables). I
am not sure that the Latin proverb *We lose the certain
things, while we seek the uncertain ones* (Certa amitti-
mus, dum incerta petimus) alludes to the fable of the
dog which lost its meat by snapping at the reflection
in the water. Possibly we have two independent expressions of the same idea, the proverb in literal and
the fable in figurative form. The beast epic gives us
When the fox preaches, beware your geese and the traditional descriptions of the Land of Cockaigne, *Roast
doves fly into no one's mouth* (Gebratene Tauben flie-
gen niemand in den Mund). Possibly we may see a
parallel in "All thy strongholds shall be like fig trees
with the first ripe figs: if they be shaken, they shall
even fall into the mouth of the eater,"[1] but more
probably the Biblical passage serves merely to illustrate how obvious the figure is. In a similar way, the
ass playing the lute or, as in Boethius and Chaucer,
the harp, was a proverbial symbol for impossibilities

---

[1] *Nahum* iii, 12. Quitard regards this passage as source; see p. 37. Compare Büchmann as above, p. 84.

and is perhaps derived from some comparison involving or implying an impossibility rather than from a specific narrative. There are other allusions which cannot be referred to a definite fable and which can perhaps be better interpreted as allusions to such vividly conceived scenes as we have been describing: the Roman proverbial exclamation "Asinus de Aesopi puteo!" was used on seeing an unexpected person whose outcry disturbs everyone, and Petronius says "The ass on the roof" (Asinus in tegulis) of an unheard-of, ominous event; but in neither case do we fully understand the allusion.

Perhaps *One swallow does not make a summer* is associated with a story, but the suggested relationship is different from that exemplified by the proverbs already mentioned. A youth squandered his inheritance and, when he saw the first swallow, sold his cloak. But it turned cold and the swallow died, whereupon the youth, who was suffering from the cold, cried, "One swallow does not make a summer." Possibly the longest and most curious history of a proverb arising from a narrative is that of Αἴξ (var. Οἶς) τὴν μάχαιραν ('The goat [var. the sheep], the knife').[1] When a goat was about to be sacrificed, no knife could be found. But the pawing of the animal revealed a knife in the ground and the sacrifice was carried out. The story has Arabic and even Hindu

1 Wesselski, *Erlesenes* (Gesellschaft Deutscher Bücherfreunde in Böhmen, VIII, Prague, 1928), p. 98.

parallels. In a curious Italian form of the proverb a hen replaces the goat or sheep. We might regard this as merely a casual substitution, but Wesselski, who studies the history of the fable and the proverb exhaustively, shows that it arises from the misunderstanding of a Spanish word.

In several instances we can suppose that a story lies behind a proverb, although we can no longer identify it: *A fool would take the song of the cuckoo for the music of the harp* (Ein tore næme des gouches sanc für den süezen harpfen klanc); *Those who eat cherries with great lords shall have their eyes sprinted out with the stones.* Possibly a connection with the fairy-tale of the Frog-Prince (Grimm, No. 1; Aarne-Thompson, No. 440) may be seen in *He who was a frog is now king* (Qui fuit rana, nunc est rex) and *If one loves a frog, one thinks the frog to be Diana* (Si quis amat ranam, ranam putat esse Dianam); but it is at best doubtful.

There are, we may note in passing, examples of reverse process: a proverb is turned into a tale. Odo of Cheriton, who versified Latin fables in twelfth-century England, turned *Do not throw pearls before swine* (Neque mittatis margaritas vestras ante porcos, *Matt.* vii, 6) into a dull story, and also *The cat would eat fish but will not wet her feet.*[1] According to Otto, the author of the standard collection of Latin proverbs, the proverb *The mountains give birth, a ridiculous*

1 For these and other examples see Voigt, *Zeitschrift für Deutsches Altertum*, XXIII (1879), 294 (No. 30*a*), 305 (No. 11), 287 (No. 14), 301 (No. 58), 304 (No. 8).

mouse is born (Parturiunt montes, ridiculus mus nascetur) preceded the story. The proverb is definitely Greek in origin, if we may trust the allusions in Latin writers; and it is referred to as a proverb, not a fable. The fable, which is first found in Phaedrus, is never mentioned in Greek. Under the circumstances the precedence of the proverb over the fable seems reasonably clear. In the same connection [1] Otto contradicts himself in regard to the proverbial phrase "to nurse a viper in one's breast," which is, he maintains on one occasion, older than the fable in Phaedrus and, on another, younger. Perhaps the best example is the old saying *For the want of a nail the shoe was lost; for the want of a shoe the horse was lost; for the want of a horse the rider was lost; for the want of a rider the battle was lost; and all for the want of a horseshoe nail.* Expanded into a narrative, this saying has found a place in the *Household Tales* of the Brothers Grimm.

The development of fables from proverbs is readily understood when we stop to think how easily a story could spring from *A bull in a china shop.* Yet in many cases it is difficult to determine which came first. Whenever the scanty narrative content of the fable is summed up in the proverb, we are justified in suspecting that the fable is secondary in origin. Thus,

---

1 *Sprichwörter*, p. xxv, where additional examples are given. He also believes that *They have put a saddle on the ox; it is no task for me* (Clitellae bovi sunt impositae plane, non est nostrum onus) is an allusion to a fable; cf. p. 262 and *Archiv für Lateinische Lexikographie,* VI (1889), 9 n. 1.

the Italian *I am not the lamb Pecorella which loses a mouthful because it says "Baa!"* (Io non son Pecorella che perde il buccone per dire Umbè) has so little narrative substance that we need hardly invent a fable as a source. Similarly, *"Look at his hands and not at his eyes," said the bird* ("Pongli mente alli mani, e non a gli occhi," disse l'uccellino) contains all that is essential in the fable of the bird-catcher whose eyes fill with tears from the cold while he wrings the necks of the birds. The fable which can be positively recognized as the source of a proverb appears in its proverbial dress as an allusion, intelligible to those familiar with the story, and not as a summary, e. g. *Sour grapes; Dog in the manger; Ass in a lion's skin.*

Proverbs and Folk-verse

The very curious and interesting relations of certain proverbs to some simple and primitive forms of verse have never been cleared up satisfactorily.[1] Obviously such a proverb as *Auch rote Äpfel sind wurmstichig* ('Even red apples are wormy') stands in some intimate connection with a widely sung quatrain, which is reported as early as 1613:

---

1 See K. Euling, *Das Priamel bis Hans Rosenplüt* (Germanistische Abhandlungen, No. 25), p. 179 n. 3; Strack, *Hessische Blätter für Volkskunde*, II (1903), 69, 174; *Die Österreich-Ungarische Monarchie in Wort und Bild* (Vienna, 1891), VIII (Kärnten und Krain), 151; A. Kopp, *Ein Sträusschen Liebesblüten im Garten Deutscher Volksdichtung Gepflückt* (Leipzig, 1902), No. 19. See also the interesting remarks in the preface to D. Hyde, *Songs of Connacht* (Dublin, n. d.). Apparently a literary tradition lies behind the metrical form of certain Irish proverbs.

Es ist kein Apfel so rosenrot,
es steckt ein Kernlein drin;
es war keine Jungfrau nie so schön,
sie trägt einen falschen Sinn.[1]

Some have maintained that the proverb came before the quatrain; others, who declare that the germ of all poetry is the strophe and not the line, have zealously defended the contrary opinion. Certainly such matters are not to be decided on the basis of doctrinaire notions of primitive poetry. The old proverb *When it rains, it becomes wet* (Wenn es regnet, wird es nass), which is known in Old High German, is found in *Schnaderhüpfel*, the quatrains sung so widely in southern Germany and the Tyrol, and in the first stanza of a children's song, but no one has suggested that the songs are older than the proverb. Machado y Alvarez collects a few examples of proverbs occurring in similar Spanish quatrains ("coplas") and offers some general comment without reaching a decision.[2] Further discussion of the evidence is not very likely to bring us closer to the origins of poetry, but we may learn to understand better the interrelations of certain proverbs and traditional verses. The situation is perhaps a little different where improvisation in verse is extremely easy. A distinction between proverbs,

1 Wander, *Deutsches Sprichwörter-Lexikon* (Leipzig, 1867–80), *s. v.* Apfel, 6; Kopp, as above; Strack, as above, II, 174.
2 *Estudios sobre Literatura Popular* (Biblioteca de las Tradiciones Populares, Vol. V [Sevilla, 1884]), pp. 67–71, "Coplas sentenciosas," pp. 75–79, "Antinomia entre un refrán y una copla."

short lyrics, and charms is not always readily made,
and the forms flow into one another.[1]

Proverbs and Individual Authors [2]

Of course an individual creates a proverb and sets
it in circulation. The inventor's title to his property
may be recognized by all who use it or his title may be
so obscured by the passage of time that only investigation will determine the source of the saying. No
one disputes Shakespere's claim to *To be or not to be*,
but Sir Francis Bacon has not maintained his hold on
Knowledge is power with equal success. We must also
consider the many instances of faulty or erroneous
ascription. The works of ready reference which deal
with all these problems in "familiar quotations" or,
as the Germans say, "winged words" (geflügelte
Worte) are invaluable in proverb study.

1 See, for example, Krohn, "Die Entwicklung eines Sprichwortes zum
Lyrischen Liede," *Mélanges en l'Honneur de Vaclav Tille* (Prague,
1929), pp. 109–112.
2 See the bibliography of collections of familiar quotations in Büchmann, *Geflügelte Worte* (Leipzig, 1912), p. xxvi. The more important
collections are Arlaud, *Bevingede Ord* (Copenhagen, 1878); Bartlett,
Familiar Quotations (Boston, 1924); Benham, *Book of Quotations,
Proverbs, and Household Words* (London, 1924); Alexandre, *Musée
de la Conversation* (Paris, 1902); Büchmann, *Geflügelte Worte; der
Citatenschatz des Deutschen Volkes* (Leipzig, 1864, 1920); Nehry,
Citatenschatz, Geflügelte Worte, Sprichwörter und Sentenzen (Leipzig,
1889); Winter, *Unbeflügelte Worte* (Augsburg, 1888); Fumagalli, *Chi
l'ha detto? Reportorio Metodico e Ragionato di 1575 Citazioni e Frasi di
Origine Letteraria* (Milan, 1895); Otto, *Die Sprichwörter und Sprichwörtlichen Redensarten der Römer* (Leipzig, 1890); Curti, *Schweizer
Geflügelte Worte* (Zurich, 1896); Ahnfelt, *Bevingade Ord* (Stockholm,
1879).

At the very beginning of a proverb's history there is obviously no question of "communal composition," although the acceptance or rejection by tradition which follows immediately upon the creation of the proverb is a factor in its making quite as important as the first act of invention. Oliver Wendell Holmes, if I am not mistaken, expresses the idea more simply thus: "Next the originator of a good saying is the first quoter of it." In Germanic proverbs Heusler [1] recognizes two strata of different ages. The older proverbs reflect the mood and literary style of the Viking Age; the younger proverbs deal with household life and show a resignation and whimsical humor which are entirely new. The differences arise not solely from the passing of the viking but also from the fact that the genre has fallen into the hands of the peasant and the common man. This explanation, if it is correct, involves a descent of literary and intellectual goods and fashions from one social level to another on a large scale. Of course we cannot hope to reach back to individual authors in contemplating this process, but the process does imply clearly a person and not a group as the starting point. We may perhaps see something analogous to the development which Heusler describes in *Faint heart ne'er won fair lady*. Although this is an old proverb, it was never, I suppose, vulgar and colloquial. Neither the language nor the

---

[1] *Altgermanische Dichtung* (Handbuch der Literaturwissenschaft, Wildpark-Potsdam, 1923), p. 68, § 61.

figure suggests the peasant. *Love 'em and leave 'em* is more in the vulgar mood, although it smells of the vaudeville stage and thus bespeaks a sophisticated origin.

A few proverbs can be assigned to definite authors with a reasonable degree of confidence. Naturally our assurance becomes less and less, the farther back we must go to find the source or the inventor. Many such proverbs are of course Biblical or classical and will be taken up later. Here we need cite only a few instances of proverbs which can be traced to particular persons. According to his saga, Ragnar Loðbrókr said, "Gnyðia mundu nu grisir, ef þeir visse, hvat enn gamle þyldi" ('The pigs would grunt now, if they knew what the old one suffers'), when he was in the snake-pit. The sentence, which implies an allusion to a particular situation and cannot be a metaphor from daily life, has become proverbial in the Scandinavian languages: the Swedish *Grisarna skulle grymta om de visste vad galten lider* ('The little pigs would grunt, if they knew what the boar was suffering') may serve as an example.[1] Petrarch created the apothegm *A good death does honor to a whole life* (Un bel morir tutta la vita onora, *Canz.*, xvi, st. 5, ll. 12–13), which was widely used in later Italian literature.[2] It was in the nature of things that Petrarch's apothegm should call

1 *Ragnarssaga Loðbroka*, 15; Kock and Petersen, *Ostnordiska och Latinska Medeltidsordspråk* (Copenhagen, 1889–94), II, 194; Bugge, *Arkiv för Nordisk Filologi*, X (1894), 96.
2 Wesselski, *Angelo Polizianos Tagebuch* (Leipzig, 1929), p. 45, No. 96.

forth a burlesque version: *A good flight saves life again*
(Un bel fuggir salva la vita ancora).[1] We are indebted
to Francis Bacon for *Knowledge is power*. *God tempers
the wind to the shorn lamb* is ordinarily credited to
Sterne, but before him it had a long history in France.
Perhaps the proverb was introduced into England by
George Herbert in the *Jacula Prudentum*. *To err is
human; to forgive divine* is a literary proverb invented
by Pope. *Three removes are worse than a fire* may be
Benjamin Franklin's. Possibly Robespierre fathered
Omelets are not made without breaking eggs. Lincoln
said, *Don't swap horses in the middle of a stream*. It is
generally believed that he was inventing the proverb,
although it is possible that he was merely using one
that was already current. *Verify your references* is a
scholar's maxim which tradition assigns to Routh,
Jowett, and Skeat. *The bigger they come, the harder
they fall* is the property of James J. Corbett. The
warning *Don't sell America short*, which is often said
to have been uttered by J. Pierpont Morgan, was
probably, according to the belief of those associated
with the firm, first voiced by his father, Junius
Spencer Morgan, when in business in London. It was
couched in the technical language of the time as *Do
not sell a bear on the United States*. J. Pierpont Morgan
adapted it to the idiom of Wall Street. A new proverb
took form when he rejected the proposal to dissolve
the trusts with *You can't unscramble eggs*.

1 Wesselski, *Angelo Polizianos Tagebuch* (Leipzig, 1929), p. 45, No. 96.

Conceivably a proverb may for a time be associated with the inventor's name, although all ascriptions to definite persons must be looked upon with suspicion. So old a proverb as *Know thyself* is variously assigned to Thales, Chilon, Solon, Bias, Phemonoe, "through whom the Pythian God is said to have first distributed favors to men," Phanothea, the priestess of Delphi, and the Delphic oracle. It no doubt owes much of its wide circulation to its use as an inscription in the temple of Delphic Apollo. Certainly a significant indication of its proverbial nature lies in the fact that it is credited to so many sources; furthermore, we must hesitate in assigning it to any one of them. Erasmus can scarcely be right in finding the source of *What is bred in the bone will not out of the flesh* in Horace. He is, of course, referring to "Drive out nature with a fork,[1] it will come back nevertheless" (Naturam expellas furca, tamen usque recurret, *Ep.*, i, 10, 24); but in this we have the idea and not the form of the modern proverb. The illustration shows how much care must be exercised in ascribing proverbs to definite persons and sources. *Verify your references* is perhaps nowhere more in place than in such matters.

A few more examples will show the nature of such ascriptions of proverbs.[2] When St. Jerome quotes the

1 This may mean a pitchfork or a fork used to punish slaves.
2 Compare the examples of Latin quotations which verge on proverbs: Otto, *Sprichwörter*, p. xxii; Otto, *Die Geflügelten Worte bei den Römern*

remark of Epicharmus (or Pittacus), "When they do not know how to talk, they cannot keep silence" (Cum loqui nesciant, tacere non possunt), and characterizes it as an old saw (vetus proverbium), we need not for a moment hesitate to accept his characterization, although the uncertainty as to the author casts doubt on the correctness of any ascription. *Like a fish out of water* (Sicut piscis sine aqua caret vita, ita sine monasterio monachus) is attributed to a Pope Eugenius, but it is found in Sozomen's *Ecclesiastical History* and still earlier in a life (not later than A.D. 373) of St. Anthony ascribed to St. Athanasius. The Irish *Better old debts than old grudges* is declared to belong to Prince Aldfrid, son of Oswy, King of Northumbria, and, with a slight variation, to Fíthal, lawgiver to King Cormac macAirt. Probably the most interesting of all such ascriptions is that of

> Wer nicht liebt Wein, Weib und Gesang,
> Der bleibt ein Narr sein Lebelang.

> ('He who does not love wine, women, and song
> Is a fool all his life long.')

This saying is generally credited to Martin Luther, but except for one of his remarks at table — and it is not directly parallel — there is no ascription to him before 1775. Nor is there any good reason for believing that Louis XIV ever said "L'état c'est moi

(Breslau, 1890). See in general the many handbooks of familiar quotations, of which the most useful and most accurate is Büchmann, *Geflügelte Worte* (Berlin, 1920).

(I am the state)," even though it is often assigned to a speech before the French parliament on April 13, 1655.[1] The international proverb *Sunt tria damna domus: imber, mala femina, fumus* ('There are three accursed things in a house: dripping, an evil woman, smoke'), which Pope Innocent III recast, is assigned with some show of justice to Solomon, but Aristotle cannot rightfully claim it. Nor did Plato ever say *Homo proponit, Deus disponit* or anything similar, although the *Vision of Piers Plowman* gives him that honor. Figures about whom traditions of wisdom have gathered attract proverbs to themselves in the same way that jests collect about Eulenspiegel and Joe Miller.

The incidents narrated to explain the origins of proverbs are often curious, and, so far as authenticity is concerned, must be classed with the ascriptions of proverbs to definite persons. In some instances, the story, like the ascription, may rest on fact; in others, the narrative has been made *ad hoc*. Generally speaking, we cannot hope to control the truth of either story or ascription. The explanation, for example, that *When in Rome, do as the Romans do* takes its rise in a conversation of St. Ambrose with St. Augustine may be correct, but we cannot be sure. St. Augustine, the story goes, had found that the Romans did not fast on the day to which he had been accustomed at Milan. He asked St. Ambrose on what day he should

1 Büchmann, *Geflügelte Worte* (Leipzig, 1920), p. 456.

fast, and received as answer, "When I am here, I do not fast on the Sabbath; when I am at Rome, I fast on the Sabbath. To whatever church you come, observe its practice, if you do not wish to suffer or to create a scandal." It is important to note that the actual words of the proverb are not used by either saint; hence the proverb is not a direct quotation. Yet it sums up the situation and the moral in pregnant words.) A similar condensation is probably seen in *Vox populi, vox Dei* ('The voice of the people, the voice of God'), for which no exactly corresponding source exists. The famous maxim *The end justifies the means* is, I suspect, open to a similar explanation, for the Jesuit motto *Exitus actus probat* will scarcely suffice as a source. And I cannot refrain from mentioning here the famous phrase *Das Volk dichtet* (The folk composes poetry), which bears within itself the Romantic doctrines of poetic origins. Although it is usually fathered on Jacob Grimm, no one has found a source for it nearer than "das dichtende Volk." The very creation of the direct, effective form *Das Volk dichtet* out of an inferior form is an illustration of the process of poetic origins.

But to return to our muttons: the stories told to explain the origin of proverbs are often not worthy of credence. Possibly Pliny is narrating an actual occurrence when he explains the origin of *Shoemaker, stick to your last!* When Apelles had painted a picture, he displayed it for public criticism and hid where

he might hear the comments. The remarks made by
a cobbler were too sharp for the painter to bear and
he burst forth, saying, "Shoemaker, stick to your
last!" Perhaps Apelles was using a familiar proverb;
perhaps he coined it for this occasion. A famous
Greek story and myth is told to explain the origin of
There's many a slip 'twixt cup and lip: a slave whom
his master had treated with great cruelty prophesied
that the master should never live to drink wine from
the vineyard in which he was working. When the
wine was ready, the master taunted the slave and
forced him to hold the cup. But before the cup was
tasted word came that a boar was laying waste the
vineyard; the master hastened to kill the boar and
was killed in the encounter. Hence the Greek proverb, *Many things find place between the cup and lip.*
Since this story is none other than the widely told
tale of Attis,[1] it is altogether probable that the story
originally had nothing to do with the proverb, but
was linked with it by some chance. In the same way,
the notion is quite erroneous that *A cat may look at a
king* or its variant German form, *A cat may look at an
emperor* (Darf doch die Katze den Kaiser ansehen),
takes rise in a visit (in 1517) of Maximilian I to the
shop of Hieronymus Resch, the maker of wood-cuts.
The cat which lay on the work-table looked at the
emperor suspiciously, but did not move. Hence, it is

1 See Taylor, "The Death of Orvar Oddr," *Modern Philology*, XIX
(1921), 93–106.

said, came the proverb. The date of the emperor's
visit is definitely fixed, and consequently the fact
that the proverb was printed in northern Germany in
1514 makes the traditional explanation impossible.
A French parallel, *A dog may look at a bishop* (Un
chien regarde bien un évêque), is explained as an
allusion to a prohibition formulated by the second
council of Mâcon in A.D. 585. Bishops might not keep
dogs, for if they did those who sought aid might be
bitten. The absence of any direct historical connection between the prohibition and the proverb makes
it hard to accept the explanation at its face value.
We can probably consider the French proverb a traditional variation of the English and German forms.)
Instances in which the explanation turns on old or
supposedly old manners and customs, and not on
stories, will be mentioned later.

TRANSLATED PROVERBS

Throughout the history of proverbs an abundant
source of new sayings has been translation from one
language into another. We can often recognize what
has happened by the presence of stylistic or metrical
irregularities: the translator has failed to reproduce
the symmetry and polish of the original. As regards
ultimate origins, such proverbs fall into two classes:
sayings which are actually proverbs from the beginning and therefore have come into being in one or another of the ways already described, and sayings, or-

dinarily Biblical or classical, which owe their wide currency to literary and religious associations, but have in the course of time lost connection with their origins and are recognized as proverbs like any others. Such proverbs we may call "learned," as contrasted with "popular," although the term refers only to our own more extensive knowledge and not to an essential difference in origin or kind.

Translation of proverbs from one language into another has always occurred when two languages have stood in intimate cultural relations for some length of time. For example, Latin proverbs of Greek origin are not infrequent.[1] Even *The die is cast* (Alea jacta est) is probably Greek: Pompey tells us that Caesar spoke the Greek words on crossing the Rubicon.[2] *Love cures the very wound it makes* (Amoris vulnus idem sanat) is Greek, too, and Tertullian's *Nihil enim ad Andromachen* ('That has nothing to do with the case' [an English proverb, ultimately a quotation from Gilbert and Sullivan's operetta, *The Mikado*]). *A rolling stone gathers no moss* is said to be a Greek proverb recorded by Lucian, which is the source of a mediaeval Latin proverb, *Saxum volutum non obducitur musco*.

No one has attempted, so far as I am aware, to define the extent and nature of Latin borrowings of

---

1 See in general Otto, p. xxii.
2 Since the Greek proverb employs the imperative, Erasmus is very likely justified in correcting the Latin to read "Let the die be cast" (Alea jacta esto).

Greek proverbs.[1] Obviously the incompleteness of the record and the inconvenience of bringing together the Greek sources make such a study difficult, but the situation is no more discouraging than in many another investigation in classical philology. Among the possible foreign influences of Latin proverbs we need consider only the Greek, for the two Punic proverbs, one from classical Latin and one preserved for us by St. Augustine, will scarcely provide a basis for speculation. In Latin proverbs of Greek origin we perceive more or less clearly three degrees of adaptation to the new surroundings: (1) complete acceptance by the folk, (2) deliberate employment of a foreign proverb, (3) casual and fumbling translation. Among these we cannot always distinguish with ease and confidence. The retention of a proverb by the Romance peoples, if we could always recognize it as retention and distinguish it from later learned borrowing from the classics, could be used to identify and define classical Latin proverbs which had fully established themselves in oral tradition. The existence of Greek proverbs of Latin origin is doubtful.[2] An exhaustive study of the problems involved in these relations of Latin and Greek culture would apparently be profitable. Only experience will show what obstacles lie in the way of solving this and similar problems which turn

1 Crusius makes some helpful remarks on this problem in his review of Otto, *Wochenschrift für Klassische Philologie*, VIII (1891), coll. 428–429. See also Otto, pp. xviii–xix.
2 See Otto, pp. xviii–xix; Crusius, as above, col. 426.

on the borrowing and translating of proverbs. The bravest effort in this direction is Altenkirch's comparison [1] of Greek and Slavic proverbs, but in the choice of subject we cannot limit ourselves so strictly as he thinks necessary. He demands that one of the two proverbial stocks compared should have been recorded before cultural contacts had begun. Of course such a limitation facilitates the comparison, but it is rarely present. As he points out, we must also be on our guard lest we compare analogous proverbs which are nevertheless of entirely independent origin. He does not consider the possibility of stylistic criteria as standards in determining the nature and direction of these cultural currents.

A particularly interesting question presents itself in connection with certain medieval Latin proverbs associated with vernacular proverbs. In collections from widely separated places we find the same Latin versions; e. g. *Passere sub tecto remanente recedit yrundo* ('While the sparrow remains under the eaves, the swallow departs') appears in a thirteenth-century Vienna manuscript, a fifteenth-century Basel manuscript of probably Low Franconian (Dutch) provenience, and, for the first time with the vernacular original, in the Dutch and Latin *Proverbia communia sive seriosa* of the end of the fifteenth century, and no doubt in many other places. *Qui tenet anguillam per*

---

1 " Die Beziehungen zwischen Slaven und Griechen in ihren Sprichwörtern," *Archiv für Slavische Philologie*, XXX (1909), 1–47, 321–364.

caudam, non habet illam ('He who holds an eel by the tail does not have it') occurs in the same Vienna and Basel manuscripts and persists in several printed collections of the end of the sixteenth century, so tenacious is the tradition when once established. *Sub nive quod tegitur, dum nix perit, omne videtur* ('All is seen that is hidden under the snow, when the snow melts') is in the Basel manuscript and the *Proverbia communia*. Probably we have enough instances to discover the history of some important mediaeval manuscript collections. Voigt believes, for example, that the rather large collection which he prints under the title *Florilegium Gottingense* contains traces of earlier (perhaps lost) alphabetical collections. Careful comparisons might disclose the history and interrelations of proverb collections just as such comparisons have already clarified the history of glosses.

But to return to the subject of the translation of proverbs. In the flood tide after the Middle Ages, with the Renaissance and the publication in 1500 of Erasmus' *Veterum Maximeque Insignium Paroemiarum, id est Adagiorum Collectanea*, although it was only a thin book of 152 pages, the translation of proverbs from one language into another becomes rampant and everywhere enriches the national stocks of proverbs. Translation has always been an important means of enlarging a nation's proverbial stores, but the systematic manner in which such translations were made in the period following the

Renaissance creates new problems. In the countries where several collections were printed in the course of the sixteenth century, notably in Germany, it is possible to see and study the gradual acclimatization of a proverb. One translation after another is tried and rejected, until finally some form gains general acceptance.

We have a clear and satisfactory description of this process in Jente's history of *Morgenstunde hat Gold im Munde* ('The morning hour has gold in its mouth').[1] In the sixteenth century, collectors struggled with the translation of the humanistic proverb *Aurora Musis amica* ('The dawn a friend to the Muses'), which is first used by Erasmus in a letter of 1497 to Christian Northoff of Lübeck and first printed in his *Colloquies* of 1518. Apparently the need for a translation did not arise before the end of the century, since neither Johannes Agricola (1529) nor Sebastian Frank (1541) in their large collections, which give much space to classical and humanistic materials, mentions either original or translation. At first, we have a clumsy paraphrase, which by its ineptitude suggests the probability that no briefer and better form existed. A translation of 1576, the oldest of all known translations, is to the following effect:

1 "'Morgenstunde hat Gold im Munde,'" *Publications Modern Language Association*, XLII (1927), 865–872; see some additional material in Stoett, *Nederlandsche Spreekwoorden* (Zutphen, 1924–25), *s. v.* Morgenstond.

Aurora amica Musis.
Surgere non cesses, cum Phoebus surgit ab ortu:
Mane bonis studijs quilibet aptus erit.
Welcher begert zstudieren wol,
An morgen er frü auffstehen soll.

A few years later a better form appeared, *Die Mor-
genstundt hat die Arbeyt im Mundt* (1582), and at almost the same time *Die Morgenstunde hat Gold im
Munde* (1585) entered the lists. The variant *Die
Morgenstund hat das Brod im Mund* is found sporadi-
cally after 1605. The collections of the seventeenth
century contain one or more of these variant forms.
It is nearly a century before the competition is definitely settled in favor of *Morgenstunde hat Gold im
Munde*. This explanation of the development is supported by the late appearance of the proverb in the
Netherlands and Scandinavia. It is striking that the
unsuccessful forms had difficulty in crossing the bor-
ders of Germany: *Morgenstund har Brød i Mund* is
found once in Danish. But even the accepted form
never firmly established itself in these adjoining
countries, so closely bound to Germany by cultural
and linguistic ties. In view of this history we cannot
any longer give ear to those explanations which see
traces of Germanic myth in the proverb. Nor need we
linger over the explanation that an etymological pun,
Aurora quia habet aurum in ore, is involved. The pun
was invented long after *Morgenstunde hat Gold im
Munde* had come into being. The situation we have

just described exists in other proverbs. In *Inter os et offam* and *Inter manus et mentum*, classical Latin possessed two competing translations of the Greek proverb analogous to *There's many a slip 'twixt cup and lip*.

In later periods the problems of translation from one language into another and of borrowing from one culture by another are of course far more complex than in classical antiquity. True enough, the apparent simplicity of these problems in Latin and Greek tradition may arise from our ignorance of many factors. However this may be, it is certain that problems involving the dissemination of proverbs by translation are very complex after the Renaissance. Yet it is worth while pointing out that they are not necessarily insoluble. There are, for example, two readily distinguishable proverbs comparing the dangers of fire, water, and woman. Each has its own history. One form, *Sunt tria damna domus: imber, mala femina, fumus* ('There are three accursed things in the house: leaking, an evil woman, smoke'), which is ultimately Biblical in origin, has spread over the part of the world directly under the influence of the Latin church. Another form, *The sea, fire, woman: three evils*, is Greek in its beginnings and is disseminated by humanistic means. Only in Italy do we find the slightest signs of confusion and contamination between the two forms.

In studying the dissemination of proverbs during

the Middle Ages and later, we shall have to pay particular attention to a large and important group of
proverbs which Seiler calls "international mediaeval"
(gemeinmittelalterlich). Although they are very
widely known and form indeed a significant part of
our everyday stock, we cannot assign their origin to
one country or language; and it is doubtful whether
we shall ever know more than we do now about the
place, time, and circumstances of their invention.
Often they are found first in Latin, and evidently owe
their wide currency to this international language of
the Middle Ages. Occasionally, but much less frequently, their first appearance is in one of the mediaeval vernacular collections of maxims and sententious
observations, such as Freidank's *Bescheidenheit*. We
know little or nothing about the origin of such proverbs as *What the eye sees not, the heart rues not*; *All is
not gold that glitters*; *Give him an inch and he'll take an
ell*; *New brooms sweep clean*; *Rome was not built in a
day*; *It's an ill bird that fouls its own nest*; *Strike while
the iron is hot*. To the same class of materials belongs
the distich

> When the Devil was sick, the Devil a monk would be;
> When the Devil was well, the Devil a monk was he.

The rhyme has circulated since the early Middle Ages
in Latin, French, English, German, and no doubt
other languages as well. Luther and Melanchthon did
not disdain to cite it, and *Joe Miller's Complete Jest
Book* preserves it for us. The more exact definition of

what constitutes the stock of international mediaeval proverbs is perhaps the most important and extensive task in the whole field. Only when the stock of such proverbs is known and their history written, can we progress to the more special examination of individual national stocks.

BIBLICAL PROVERBS [1]

Two classes of materials, the Biblical and the classical, have quite naturally contributed a far larger share of translated proverbs than any other source. In all the centuries of the Christian Era the Bible, in which were included the Apocrypha and, notably, the book of Ecclesiasticus or Sirach, was an obvious and inexhaustible source. The Church Fathers quoted

1 The special character of Biblical proverbs makes it possible to use collections and studies in any language. The more important reference works for such proverbs are found in Dutch and German: Kat, *Bijbelsche Uitdrukkingen en Spreekwijzen in onze Taal* (Zutphen, 1926); Laurillard, *Bijbel en Volkstaal* (Amsterdam, 1875; 2d ed., Rotterdam, 1901), with the comments by Harrebomée, *Bedenkingen op het Prijsschrift van Dr. E. Laurillard* (Gorinchem, 1877); Sprenger van Eijk, *Handleiding tot de Kennis van onze Vaderlandsche Spreekwoorden* (Rotterdam, 1835–41); Zeeman, *Nederlandsche Spreekwoorden . . . aan den Bijbel Ontleend* (Dordrecht, 1877, 1888); and Schulze, *Die Biblischen Sprichwörter der Deutschen Sprache* (Göttingen, 1860); Büchmann, *Geflügelte Worte* (Berlin, 1920), pp. 1–70. Biblical quotations and allusions in Old and Middle English literature are collected by A. S. Cook (*Biblical Quotations in Old English Prose Writers* [New York, 1898–1903]) and Mary W. Smyth (*Biblical Quotations in Old English before 1350* [New York, 1911]); although these books are not primarily concerned with proverbial materials, they give an idea of the way in which the Bible was used and how Biblical proverbs may have arisen. Marvin (*Curiosities in Proverbs* [New York, 1916]) gives some miscellaneous and unsystematic notes on English Biblical proverbs.

and reshaped in more pregnant form the words of Biblical wisdom. A little later the efforts to provide translations of the Bible or of individual books in the different modern languages poured out a steady stream of material which was either proverbial or capable of being made proverbial by slight adaptation. Classical sources did not flow so abundantly, although from the very beginning of Christian history classical admonitions united with Christian maxims in colloquial and formal discourse. A new and stronger current of classical influence sets in with Humanism and the Renaissance.

Although proverbs of Biblical origin have often been collected, they have never been studied as examples of the history and development of oral tradition. The books which deal with them indicate, although unfortunately not always with accuracy, the Biblical passages which have become current among the folk. The author, often swayed by his didactic desires, includes an apothegm which he thinks ought to be a proverb. These books do not usually discuss what kinds of Biblical passages succeed in establishing themselves, what changes occur in these quotations during their lives on the lips of the folk, or what quotations are most exposed to changes. Such books do not often seek to identify the exact source of the quotation. A slight variation from the Biblical phrase — a variation to which, however, the proverb often clings tenaciously — may tell us that it is derived from one of the Church Fathers, a mediaeval preacher, or an obsolete translation of the Bible rather than the so-called King James Version or some other received text.

In proverbs of Biblical origin we see all stages of the disintegration of a phrase: the Biblical quotation gradually becomes a vague, inaccurate reminiscence. The Biblical "A living dog is better than a dead lion" (Melior est canis vivus leone mortuo, *Eccles.* ix, 4) has, for example, suffered little alteration. Indeed, the lack of freedom in its use and the bookish atmosphere in which it seems most at home makes one inclined to regard it as a learned or semi-learned phrase which has never quite become a popular proverb. A characteristic alteration is seen in the popular forms of the Biblical "Every one that doeth evil hateth the light" (Omnis enim, qui male agit, odit lucem, *John* iii, 20). It exists as a simple quotation from the Bible in the Elizabethan *He that doeth evil, hateth the light*. Earlier than this, about the end of the fifteenth century we find on the continent *The evil one avoids the light as the Devil the Cross* (Die quade schuwet dat licht als die duvel dat cruce), with a Latin translation, *Demon ipse crucem fugit ut malus undique lucem*. The comparison with the Devil, which is apparently a mediaeval invention and addition, is a typical modification of a Biblical proverb: the maxim is made more effective by a picturesque and vividly conceived scene. No particular form of this proverb seems to have definitely established itself in the European proverbial

stock. Another characteristic development is seen in
Money is the root of all evil, which has sprung from
"The love of money is the root of all evil" (Radix
enim omnium malorum est cupiditas, *I Tim.* vi, 10).
The shift from the abstract to the concrete adapts the
sententious apothegm into the direct and suggestive
proverb. We have the same sort of thing in *Pride
goes before a fall*, which derives immediately from
"Pride goeth before destruction, and an haughty
spirit before a fall" (Contritionem praecedit superbia
et ante ruinam exaltatur superbus, *Prov.* xvi, 18).
Once the substitution of "fall" for "destruction" had
occurred, the forces of parallelism and contrast could
create *Pride goes before and shame comes after*. The
scene is conceived still more vividly in the Swedish
Where sin drives, shame sits in the back seat (Där
odygd åker fram, sitter i baksätet skam).

There are many proverbs which do not show such
obvious and unmistakable relations to the Biblical
sources as those mentioned thus far. *Man proposes,
but God disposes* has a long history which probably
begins with "A man's heart deviseth his way: but the
Lord directeth his steps" (Cor hominis disponit viam
suam: sed Domini est dirigere gressus eius, *Prov.* xvi,
9). In the eighth century Alcuin knew "Homo cogitat, Deus iudicat" and in the twelfth, Ordericus Vita-
lis, the chronicler, has "Homo cogitat, Deus ordinat."
The characteristic rhyming form we find in the *Im-
itatio Christi*, i, 19: "Homo proponit, Deus disponit."
It is interesting to see that German, although un-

able to use the rhyming Latin form or its derivatives, has nevertheless invented a rhyming form of its
own: *Der Mensch denkt, Gott lenkt*. The most recent
development seems to be the insertion of the word
but, in this way implying the plans of God and man
are at cross-purposes. The implication, although
vaguely present in the older forms, is not directly
expressed. A proverb which diverges far from its
Biblical source is *The more he has, the more he wants*,
which may conceivably arise from "He that loveth
silver shall not be satisfied with silver; nor he that
loveth abundance with increase: this is also vanity,"
(Avarus non implebitur pecunia: et qui amat divitias,
fructum non capiet ex eis: et hos ergo vanitas, *Eccles.*
v, 9). The old proverb gives us a modern advertising
slogan: "The more you eat, the more you want"
(motto of Cracker Jack).

Occasionally we trace the origin of a Biblical proverb to a single version. Thus Luther translated "Ex
abundantia cordis os loquitur" ('Of the abundance
of the heart his mouth speaketh,' *Lk.* vi, 45; *Matt.*
xii, 34) as 'Wes das Herz voll ist, des geht der Mund
über' and defended it emphatically: "If I should follow the asses who will lay the literal words before me
and translate thus: 'From the superfluity of the heart
the mouth speaks,' tell me, is that talking German?" [1]

---

1 "Ex abundantia . . . loquitur. Wenn ich den Eseln sol folgen, die
werden mir die buchstaben furlegen, und also dolmetzschen: Auss dem
überflus des hertzen redet der mund. Sage mir, Ist das deutsch gere-
det?"— *Vom Dolmetschen* (Weimar ed., XXX, ii, 637).

Luther's form drove out the others like "Ex habitu cordis sonitus depromitur oris" ('The sound of the mouth is derived from the habit of the heart') and "Quod in cordi, hoc est in ore," which were struggling to establish themselves. Schiller, it is interesting to remember, attempted a different translation in *Wallensteins Tod*, i, 173–174:

> was der frohe Mut
> Mich sprechen liess im Überfluss des Herzens.

There is of course no question that Luther's version has fixed itself in tradition. If proof were needed, we might find it in a Swabian proverb: *Wes der Magen voll ist, läuft das Maul über* ('Whatever the stomach is full of, with that the mouth runs over'), which is made on the same model.

As a contrast, we may study the history of *Narren soll man mit Kolben lausen* ('One should louse fools with clubs'). This proverb is evidently derived from such Biblical passages as "A rod is for the back of him that is void of understanding" (Et virga in dorso eius qui indiget corde, *Prov.* x, 13); "And stripes for the backs of fools" (Et mallei percutientes stultorum corporibus, *Prov.* xix, 29); and "And a rod for the fool's back" (Et virga in dorso imprudentium, *Prov.* xxvi, 3). It established itself in its present form before the appearance of Luther's translation and persists in tradition, notwithstanding the enormous influence which so widely accepted a version must have. Luther translates the first of these passages more literally and less idiomatically as "Auf den Rücken des Narren gehört eine Rute," and, in his version, the remaining passages contain equally little suggestion of the proverb.

Direct contact with the Biblical text has not been the sole source of tradition. Where it is possible to identify the channel through which the phrase reached the folk, we can often trace it back to some compend. Quotation in preaching and in ecclesiastical writing was abundant and careless, and favored the rise of minor variations. We can at times catch a church writer in the very act of reshaping a Biblical phrase: Pope Innocent III we know to have arranged the climax "Tria sunt quae non sinunt hominem in domo permanere: fumus, stillicidium, et mala uxor" ('There are three things which do not let a man stay at home: smoke, dripping, and an evil wife'). We are not able to identify positively the inventor of *Homo proponit, Deus disponit,* but, as we have seen, its inventor, a man active in ecclesiastical life and writings, lived somewhere north of the Alps between the time of Alcuin and that of Thomas à Kempis. The limits within which the invention of *The tongue breaketh bone, though itself have none* occurred cannot be drawn so closely. Obviously it is derived from "A soft tongue breaketh the bone" (Lingua mollis confringit duritiam, *Prov.* xxv, 15) or "A blow of the tongue breaks bones" (Plaga linguae comminuet ossa, *Ecclus.* xxviii, 21) but since characteristic proverbial modifications are found both in Greek and in the languages culturally associated with Greek, like Bulgarian and Serbian, and in Latin and the vernacular languages of Western Europe, we must conclude that the transformation took place at an early time.

Biblical proverbs, and among them perhaps even those which we have discussed, may have been proverbs before their incorporation into Holy Writ. Ordinarily we are reduced to conjecture in such matters, but there are proverbs which are known to have circulated in oral tradition before their appearance in the Bible. When Our Saviour said "It is hard for thee to kick against the goad" (Durum est tibi contra stimulum calcitrare, *Acts* xxvi, 14) he was using a proverbial phrase which Pindar, Aeschylus, and Euripides knew. "Physician, heal thyself" (Medice cura teipsum, *Lk.* iv, 23) seems to have been a current proverb when the Nazarenes quoted it against Jesus as a rebuke for His having performed miracles in Capernaum and not in Nazareth. "To strain at a gnat and swallow a camel" (Caeci, excolantes culicem, camelum autem glutientes, *Matt.* xxiii, 24) we may conjecture to have been taken from popular speech, and "to eat salt with," i. e. 'to associate with,' an idiom which is still preserved in the Greek συναλιζό-μενος but is obscured in the Vulgate "convescens" (*Acts* i, 4), was an old phrase in Greek long before St. Luke used it. Nor need our illustrations be limited to the New Testament: Hosea probably did not invent the phrase "To sow the wind and reap the whirl-wind," (Quia ventum seminabunt, et turbinem me-tent, *Hosea* viii, 7). *A soft answer turneth away wrath* was known to Aeschylus as well as Solomon, and Homer used *Like will to like* before it found a place in the Book of Sirach.

Such parallel lines of tradition, the one Biblical and the other classical, are frequently found: *A friend in need is a friend indeed* goes back to Ecclesiasticus and to Ennius. Under these circumstances confusion and contamination of the two traditions is to be ex-pected, although the differences between the two forms may not always be sufficiently marked to per-mit us to differentiate them. Martha Lenschau sees a joining of Biblical and classical tradition in *Many a one falls in the snare which he has set for others* (Mancher in den Strick selbst fellt, den er andern hat gestellt). The fundamental metaphor is based on "He made a pit, and digged it, and is fallen into the ditch which he made" (Lacum aperuit, et effodit eum: et incidit in foveam, quam fecit, *Ps.* vii, 16; cf. *Prov.* xxvi, 27). She assigns the metaphor of the noose to Ovid's "They fall into the snares which they have set" (In laqueos, quos posuere, cadant, *Art. amat.*, i, 646) and other similar passages in classical authors. Martin Luther, she concludes, established the ex-pression with "pit"; the texts with "snare," "noose," "rope," and the like are either independent inven-tions or derived from Latin sources. In principle, this explanation is correct, although we cannot accept it in this particular instance. The confusion of "snare" and "pit" versions must rest, at least in some measure, on "The heathen are sunk down in the pit that they made: in the net which they hid is their own foot taken. ... The wicked is snared in the work of his own hands" (Infixae sunt Gentes in interitu, quem fecerunt. In laqueo isto, quem absconderunt, comprehensus est pes eorum. ... In operibus manuum suarum comprehensus est peccator, *Ps.* ix, 15–16). St. Jerome alludes to this passage when he says: "While you do not know, you are caught with your own snare" (Dum nescis, proprio captus es laqueo). Such authorities, the Bible, the classical poet, and the Church Father, contributed to the success of the proverb and he would be brave indeed who would endeavor to assign to each his proper share.

Classical Proverbs

From classical authors tradition derives many proverbs: *Love is blind*; *Many men, many minds*; *To err is human*; *Easy come, easy go*; *Well begun is half done*; *Better late than never*; *Don't spur a willing horse*; *No sooner said than done*; *Of two evils choose the least*; *Two heads are better than one*; *The master's eye makes the horse fat*; *While there's life, there's hope*; *One swallow does not make a summer.* No particular class of proverbs goes back to Latin and Greek literature, although metaphorical proverbs are perhaps somewhat less frequent than purely sententious observations on the conduct of life. Even a proverb so difficult to translate as a play on words is turned into a different language: *Onus, honos* ('Burden, honor') becomes the German *Würden, Bürden*.

Not infrequently a proverb of classical origin runs parallel with a proverb which seems to have developed independently. Thus the German proverb *They hang the little thieves; the big ones are allowed to run* (Die kleinen Diebe hängt man, grosse lässt man laufen) is found in many collections of popular origin and is clearly a proverb belonging to the folk. There is no definite evidence connecting it with an analogous proverb displaying a thoroughly Roman spirit of law and reverence for sacred objects: "Small sacrileges are punished; great ones are celebrated by triumphs" (Sacrilegia minuta puniuntur, magna in triumphis aguntur, Seneca, *Ep.*, lxxxvii, 23), or with a proverb in Aulus Gellius about the different treatment accorded to thieves of public and private property, or with "The big thieves bear off the little one" [to be hanged?] (Οἱ μεγάλοι κλέπται τὸν μικρὸν ἀπάγουσι, Diogenes Laertius, vi, 2, 6, 45). The classical proverbs, as we see, either refer to social relations of a political or religious nature or accuse the executioners of the same crime as the criminals. Although similar to the classical parallels, the German proverb is quite distinct. The classical examples have a respectable history of their own in German collections, but are not confused with the German parallel and are characteristically associated with authors possessing a learned background. We must conclude that the German proverb is independent satiric comment on the course of the world. Its interest and significance in the eyes of a former generation are shown by the fact that it provided the subject for a legal dissertation: *Dissertatio de trito sermone proverbio: Parvi fures suspenduntur, magni dimittuntur vel in crumena puniuntur sive marsupio reconduntur* (Altdorf, 1726).[1]

Alteration by the forces of tradition occurs quite as frequently in proverbs of classical origin as in those of Biblical origin and it need not be illustrated at great length. Plautus writes "From whatever direction the wind is, the sail is turned accordingly" (Utcumque est ventus, exim velum vortitur, *Poen.*, 754), but mediaeval and modern tradition has generally preferred to say "cloak" or "mantle" instead of "sail": *One should turn his coat according to the weather* (Man soll den Mantel kehren, als das Wetter geht). Possibly the Horatian "They change their climate, not their disposition, who run beyond the sea" (Caelum, non animam mutant, qui trans mare currunt, *Ep.*, i, 11, 27) yields *If a goose flies across the sea, there comes back a quack-quack* (Fleugt ein ganss

---

1 Cited by D. Murray, *Lawyers' Merriments* (Glasgow, 1912), p. 49; C. C. Nopitsch, *Die Literatur der Sprichwörter* (Nuremberg, 1833), p. 58; Wander, *Deutsches Sprichwörter-Lexicon, s. v.* Dieb, 170.

vber mer, so kompt ein gagag wieder her), and in
variant forms we have ass, cat, crow, jackdaw, and
fool.

Of course there have been serious accidents occasionally in the passage from Latin into the modern
languages, and, furthermore, various modern proverbs have been regarded as descendants of Latin
phrases, although the context shows clearly enough
that the similarity is merely verbal and does not involve the transmission of ideas.   Virgil's "A chill
snake, lads, lurks in the grass" (Frigidus, o pueri,
latet anguis in herba, *Ecl.*, iii, 93) is not the source of
the idea in our proverb *A snake in the grass*. The saying *When the horse is stolen, lock the barn door* cannot
rest on a misunderstanding of Juvenal's words: "If in
all the world you cannot show me so abominable a
crime, I hold my peace; I will not forbid you to smite
your breast with your fists, or to pummel your face
with open palm, seeing that after so great a loss you
must close your doors, and that a household bewails
the loss of money with louder lamentations than
death" (*Sat.*, xiii, 126 ff.). The reference concerns the
Roman custom of closing doors as a sign of mourning.
It is wisest not to think of any connection between
Juvenal and the proverb and to regard the proverb as
a peasant's invention and as comparable to such sayings as *To cover the well after the child is drowned*. We
may observe in passing that the substitutions which
occur in the variants are quite in the manner of oral

tradition: for "horse" we have "cow" or "cattle" and for "lock" we have "repair." But further illustration of such substitutions is unnecessary: proverbs live the same sort of life in tradition, whatever their past history.

II

THE CONTENT OF PROVERBS

U P to this point we have been chiefly concerned
with questions of origin and historical accidents
of transmission and preservation; now we turn our
attention to content and style. The content of proverbs affords a more suitable means of classification
and more profitable subjects of study than does the
distinction between "learned" and "popular," which
we have rejected. Of course not all classifications
according to subject are fruitful. Those which are
based upon specific objects, such as collections of
proverbs concerning dogs,[1] or women,[2] or God, do not
form suggestive groups of material. But classifications which involve ideas or which bring together
proverbs belonging to a particular cultural sphere,
such as those of proverbs dealing with legal notions,
the weather, health, agriculture, shipping, and so on,
supply us with materials which reward the labor of
collecting them. Even the bull ring has its collection
of proverbs: Miguel Moliné y Roca, *Paremiografía*

1 See, e. g., A. Koskenjaakko, *Koira Suomalaisissa ynnä Virolaisissa
Sananlaskuissa* (Helsinki, 1909).
2 See the bibliography in Bonser, *Proverb Literature* (London, 1930),
pp. 430–432, Nos. 3750–3777, and C. Benzon, *Kvinden i Ordsproget*
(Copenhagen, 1907).

Taurina (Barcelona, 1888). Collections devoted to ir-
religious and harmful proverbs, such as E. Meisner's
*Ein hundert Drey- und dreyssig Gotteslästerliche, Gott-
lose, Schändliche und Schädliche, auch Unanständige,
und theils Falsche Teutsche Sprüch-Wörter, Höchst-
sträffliche Eingeschlichene Redens-Arten, Ungeziemende
Reime und Grobe Gewohnheiten* (Jena, 1705); E[ric]
P[ontoppidan]'s *Onde Ordsprog, som Fordoerver Gode
Hoeder, Igiendrevne af Guds ord* (Bad Proverbs which
ruin Good Morals, Refuted from the Word of God
[Copenhagen, 1739]), which was translated and enlarged in Swedish (Stockholm, 1777); and J. G.
Schöner's *Sprichwörter, womit sich Laue Christen Be-
helfen* (Nuremberg, 1802),[1] might seem likely at first
sight to contain curious and interesting materials, but
the authors' purpose is so exclusively didactic that
they lose themselves in moralizing and quote only an
occasional proverb as text.

CUSTOMS AND SUPERSTITIONS

Quite naturally especial interest attaches to proverbs which contain evidences of manners and customs. Several such proverbs have been already commented upon in other connections. We may here
draw attention to a few more instances in which an
old trait has been preserved. *Good wine needs no bush*
alludes to the fact that wine shops were formerly

[1] See *Catalogue des Livres Parémiologiques composant la Bibliothèque de
Ignace Bernstein* (Warsaw, 1900), Nos. 2144, 2412, 3271.

marked by a bush in the same way that the barber still displays a barber's pole. The proverb occurs in two forms, one with "bush" and one with "ivy." The latter, *The best wine needeth no ivie-bush*, appears to have the closer connections with a tradition which begins in Renaissance Latin sources. It has often been said that this proverb reaches back to classical Latin, but the evidence is flimsy. *If the cap fits, put it on* alludes to the fool's cap. The mediaeval attitude toward saints' relics — an attitude which was of fundamental importance in architecture, literature, and life — is briefly summed up in *Every priest praises his own relics* (Ein jeder Pfaff lobt sein Heiligtum). Glass rings were gifts among poor folk in the Middle Ages. The minnesinger Walther von der Vogelweide declares that the glass ring of his sweetheart is dearer to him than the gold of a queen:

Swaz si sagen, ich bin dir holt,
und nim din glesin vingerlin für einer küneginne golt.[1]

Long before the twelfth century the fragility of a glass ring was a proverbial comparison for the fragility of certain friendships: as Bishop Salomon of Constance said at the beginning of the tenth century, "Give glass to friends of glass" (Vitrei amici vitro sunt donandi). The proverb *A man is a man still, if he hath a hose on his head* is found as late as 1732 and

[1] Ed. K. Lachmann, 50, 12; see the notes in W. Wilmanns, *Walther von der Vogelweide* (4th ed. by V. Michels, Halle, 1924 [Germanistische Handbibliothek, I, 2]), p. 211; Simrock, *Gedichte Walthers*, I, 201.

may allude to some mediaeval custom or game. It may refer to a man who has no cap and wears an old stocking in its place; in other words, a man is not to be judged by his apparel, however grotesque it may be.

Proverbs do not often contain traces of superstitions, myths, or formal religion, and most instances which have been cited fail on closer examination to bear out the correctness of the interpretation. The mythological element in the eighty-odd proverbs which L. de Baecker quotes in *De la Religion du Nord de la France avant le Christianisme* (1854) reduces to almost nothing; H. Lessmann's *Der deutsche Volksmund im Lichte der Sage* (1922), which makes an even more determined effort to find traces of myths, yields as little. A typical illustration is the proverb *Morgenstunde hat Gold im Munde* (The morning hour has gold in its mouth), which has already been mentioned in other connections. It has nothing to do with a possible mythical notion that gold pieces fall from the mouth of the dawn. Proverbs occasionally mention figures of myth and tradition, but it is extremely doubtful how much reliance can be placed on such allusions as sources of mythological information. Classical Greek proverbs are supposed to mention the gods with relative frequency, while Roman proverbs avoid such figures.[1] The proverbs of primitive

[1] Otto, "Die Götter und Halbgötter im [Lateinischen] Sprichwört," *Archiv für lateinische Lexikographie*, III (1886), 207–229, 384–387.

peoples rarely mention divine personages or significant religious matters. The notion that red-headed
people are not to be trusted is a firmly established
proverb, *Rotbart nie gut ward*; but we dare not put
much trust in the explanation that it involves an
allusion to the red beard of Thor. Similarly, modern
European proverbs give us little or no idea of the
Christian God or Christian cosmology. A few proverbs show a definite Catholic tinge and are presumably older than the Reformation, e. g. *Where God does
not help, no saint avails* (Wo Gott nicht hilft, da hilft
kein Heiliger).

The Devil is the most frequently mentioned figure
from Christian cosmology, but the allusions are not
abundant or specific enough to build up a picture.
He must have a long spoon that will sup with the Devil
and *Needs must when the Devil drives* tell us very little
about popular notions of the Devil. The German
proverb *Where the Devil can't go he sends an old
woman* (var. *his grandmother*) (Wo der Teufel nicht
hinkommen kann, schickt er ein altes Weib [*var.*
seine Grossmutter]) is equally uncommunicative.
When it rains and the sun shines at the same time, the
folk say *The Devil is beating his grandmother* (var.
wife), but the mythological allusion is obscure. Its
presence, however, is hardly to be questioned, for we
have analogous expressions in many languages of
Western Europe: the French say *The Devil is marry-
ing his daughter* (Le diable marie sa fille), the Dutch,

When it rains and the sun shines, then there is a fair in Hell (Als 't regent en de zon schijnt, dan is het kermis in de hel); and in the province of Groningen, *When it rains and the sun shines, the witches are baking pancakes* (Als het regent en de zon schint, bakken de heksen pannekoeken). The German and English versions are essentially the same. The similarities and dissimilarities of these various forms do not suggest a recent borrowing from one language by another. What the fundamental form from which the versions spring may have been and what its meaning was we cannot even conjecture. It is worth remarking that these mythological allusions, and, I suspect, mythological allusions in general, occur in proverbs which contain no metaphor.

It is easier to find proverbial illustrations of superstitions than of myths and mythical figures other than the Devil. The notion that red-headed men are not to be trusted is a firmly established proverb: *A red beard was never good* (Rotbart nie gut ward), and it is frequently joined with a like warning against bearded women: *Greet a redbeard and a bearded woman from afar* (Ein roth bart vnd bärtig weib grüez von weiten). The situation is somewhat different in a sixteenth-century German proverb which warns us against certain abnormalities: *Beware of a red Italian, a white Frenchman, and a black German* (Hüt dich vor eim roten Walhen, weissen Frantzosen, und schwartzen Teutschen). *A Sunday journey is not good* ap-

pears to be Irish superstition as well as proverb. The
belief that *A whistling girl and a crowing hen will come
to no good end*, which also occurs in the form

> Whistling girls and crowing hens
> Will all (*var.* surely) come to some bad ends,

as well as in the more cheerful, contradictory version:

> Girls that whistle and hens that crow
> Will always have fun, wherever they go,

involves a superstition of international currency.
An unlicked cub preserves the old belief that bears
give birth to a mass of flesh which must be *licked into
shape*. The latter phrase, which is of course to be
understood quite literally, has found an altogether
different interpretation on the lips of the folk. Few
such phrases enjoy the metaphorical use so typical of
the proverb with ethical or moral content, e. g. *Rats
desert a sinking ship*, i. e. 'followers leave a man of
wealth and influence when his power wanes.' Of
course the danger of seeing an explanation in myth or
superstition when it does not really exist is ever
present. *The rain falls in the lap of the happy bride*
(Felici sponsae pluit in gremium) has naught to do
with the golden rain of Danaë but uses an obvious
symbolism.[1] The Italian *A woman of good family always bears a girl as her first child* (La donna di buona
razza fa sempre la prima figliata femina) [2] and the

---

1 There is another and better known proverb: *Happy is the bride the
sun shines on, and happy the corpse the rain rains on.*
2 Wesselski, *Poliziano*, p. 214.

similar Spanish *To the lucky man a daughter is first born* (Al hombre venturero la hija le nasce primero) are probably words of comfort and not proverbial superstitions.

Some superstitions circulate in a form which may be called proverbial, but we do not clearly understand why the folk preserves these particular superstitions in an unvarying form. According to Ovid, honest women did not marry in the month of May. The manner in which he says it makes it probable that the superstition was current in a rigid, proverbial form: "Mense malas Maio nubere vulgus ait" (*Fasti*, v, 490). The belief persists in similar form in German: *Im Maien gehen Huren und Buben zur Kirche*, and in English, *Marry in May, you'll rue it for aye*. Christian modifications are *Twischen Paschen* (Easter) *un Pingsten* (Pentecost) *fryen die Unseligen*, and *Marry in Lent; you'll live to repent*. The superstition that the oil or ashes of a scorpion cure its sting yields an Italian proverb: *Non mi morse mai scorpione, che io non mi medicassi col suo olio,*[1] but it can scarcely be regarded as other than a bit of traditional medical lore. *The more camomile is trodden on, the faster it grows*, which is perhaps part of the euphuistic tradition, is a stock Elizabethan comparison of unknown origin. *A woman, a dog, and a walnut tree, the more they are beaten the better they be* enjoys, on the

---

[1] Wesselski, *Erlesenes* (Gesellschaft Deutscher Bücherfreunde in Böhmen, VIII, Prague, 1928), p. 10, n. 1; Skeat, *Early English Proverbs* (Oxford, 1910), No. 117.

contrary, frequent use as a proverb, although there is no apparent reason why the walnut should be particularly favored except as a characteristic northern nut-bearing tree. There is a Spanish variant with the almond.

Allusions which are no longer understood offer extremely interesting problems and very often resist successfully all attempts at their solution. Occasionally the unexplained proverb has an international circulation, and the resulting abundance of materials, often illuminating the difficulty from various angles, ought to make solution easier. Although there are many references in various languages after the late Middle Ages to *Those who eat cherries with great lords shall have their eyes dashed out with the stones* and *If the sky falls, we shall have larks*, the proverbs are obscure. I am reminded that the European lark and the American lark are very different birds and that the European lark flies to great heights. Possibly an explanation can be found in this way. The proverb belongs, of course, to the type of "never-never" sayings.

It has been said that *Those who live in glass houses should not throw stones* rests upon a Spanish idiom according to which a "glass house" is a house with windows. If this is true, — I have not been able to find the idiom in question, — the proverb is ultimately Spanish in origin. *The game is not worth the candle* involves an unexplained allusion, perhaps to some game in which a candle was the stake or forfeit, or, as is more plausibly suggested, it refers to the fact that gamblers were required to pay for the candles to light the gambling rooms, and obviously the game was no longer worth the candle when the stakes became small. The variant *The flame is not worth the candle* illustrates a change arising in oral transmission; it cannot serve to explain the origin. *Tace is Latin for candle*, a proverbial admonition to silence, must contain a pun or allusion. *Lovers live by love as larks live by leeks* is utterly obscure, but it is hardly explicable as mere alliterative nonsense. Possibly *Every dog has his day* has some reference to dog-days, but this is more than doubtful.

The temptation to read the manners of earlier days into a proverb is one which besets every annotator, but not all explanations of the sort can be correct. Perhaps Lean, who collected a huge mass of English proverbs, is right in explaining *The weakest goes to the wall* by supposing that in households of former days the beds of the children were placed next the wall, while the father, as the strongest member of the family, slept next the door, but I am unconvinced. More probably the metaphor implies only a single bed: the child sleeps next the wall so that it will not roll out during the night. The variant explanation quoted as the words of a verger in Salisbury Cathedral may stand on its own merits: "And so, because in the old days there were no seats or pews in the nave, the cripples and old people who could not stand through the service sat on the stone bench [along the wall]: which gave rise to the saying, 'The weak went to the wall.'" Finnur Jónsson declares that the Icelandic proverb *One must honor the oak beneath which one dwells* (Verðr eik at fága, er undir skal búa, *Egilssaga*, 68, 4) alludes to the ancient custom of building houses beneath or around a large tree. If this explanation is correct, he might also have observed that the proverb can scarcely have been native to Iceland, where trees large enough to shade a house, whatever its size, would be difficult to find. In view of the parallels to the proverb, we must not think of "oak" as referring to the roof-tree. All explanations which concern themselves with cultural matters are of course greatly complicated by the familiar tendency of tradition to modernize its materials or to adapt them to local conditions. Thus the proverb which has just been discussed is found in Dutch as *Honor the tree which gives one shade* (Men nighet den boom, daer man die bate af hevet),[1] which does not necessarily allude to a tree shading a house, and consequently throws no light on the early meaning of the proverb. An extensive study of the distribution of the variant forms might determine the facts.

Like words, folk-songs, and cultural objects generally, proverbs may become old-fashioned and pass

---

1 Hoffmann von Fallersleben, *Altniederländische Sprichwörter (Proverbia communia)*, Horae Belgicae, IX (Hannover, 1854), 31, No. 486; Seiler, *Zeitschrift für Deutsche Philologie*, XLVII (1916–18), 243.

out of use. The reasons for obsolescence necessarily vary from case to case and cannot be brought under a single head: the moral lesson involved in the proverb may not seem so significant as it once did, the symbol employed may have lost its force, the essential elements of the metaphor may have ceased to be part of common experience, the language may have discarded an essential word. A systematic examination of obsolete proverbs might yield interesting results.[1] Typical proverbs that have passed out of use are *The black ox hath not trod on her foot*, i. e. 'She has not known care'; *Out of God's blessing into the warm sun*, i. e. 'from the best into something less good,' a figure which is taken, I suspect, from the scene of the congregation leaving the church. We may, and perhaps with more reason, call to mind the many and very familiar Biblical passages [2] in which shade is called desirable and regard the proverb as meaning 'from the shade into the sun.' *The hasty bitch brings forth blind whelps* and *If the sky falls, we shall have larks*, on which we have already commented, find no echo today. The oft-used Elizabethan proverb *The blind man eats many a fly* throws a flash of light on a dark corner of sixteenth-century culinary manners, and has since that time dropped out of existence. So far as the evidence goes, the proverb is English in origin and currency. A proverb which is limited in its circulation to Germany

---

1 See the chapter "Obscure Proverbs" in Marvin, *Curiosities*, pp. 52–66.
2 E. g. *Job* vii, 2; *Ps.* cxxi, 5; *Song* ii, 3; *Isa.* xxv, 4, xxxii, 2; *Jonah* iv, 6.

at the time of the Reformation is *Where the abbot pro-vides the dice, the monastery may play* (Wo der Abt die Würfel auslegt, ist's dem Konvent erlaubt zu spielen).

Just as proverbs keep memories of older manners, they may preserve words and forms which are obso-lete or are becoming obsolete, and words in meanings which are no longer used. Perhaps the most familiar illustration is *The exception proves the rule,* which is now ordinarily understood to mean 'the exception demonstrates [supports] the rule.' On the contrary, it should mean 'the exception tests the rule' (Exceptio probat regulam). We have the same meaning in the word "proof" in the saying *The proof of the pudding is in the eating.* The retention of old or obsolescent words is no doubt found in the proverbs of every lan-guage. The Romans said *Qui semel scurra, numquam pater familias* ('He who was once a man about town, is never a man of settled life') and used "scurra" in a meaning which apparently had become obsolete in classical Latin. The proverbial contrasting of "hostis" and "civis" in *Impransus non qui civem dinosceret hoste* ('He who has not had breakfast will not distinguish a citizen from a stranger') turns on the original meaning of "hostis," 'stranger.' English examples in addition to those already given are *The hailer* (receiver) *is as bad as the stailer* (thief); *When the pig is proffered, hold up the poke.* "Poke," which is now used only in English dialects, means 'bag,' and is the word from which "pocket" was formed as a diminutive.

Some explanations of old or strange words in proverbs are more ingenious than convincing. *First catch your hare* has been declared to be a misquotation from an eighteenth-century cook-book. The directions for preparing a certain dish began: "Take your hare when it is cased ('skinned') and make a pudding." Tradition, it is said, corrupted "case" to "catch" and thus altered a literal command into a metaphor from hunting. In principle, such an explanation is possible, but in this case the whole matter is set straight by a thirteenth-century proverb: *And the common folk say that it is first necessary to catch the stag and then, when it has been caught, to skin it* (Et vulgariter dicitur quod primo oportet cervum capere, et postea, cum captus fuerit, illum excoriare).[1] *A miss is as good as a mile* can scarcely find explanation in the names, Amis and Amile, of two faithful friends in mediaeval romance. The current explanation of an old and obscure German proverb *Nothing is good for the eyes* (Nichts ist gut für [*var.* ynn] die Augen) is a masterpiece of ingenuity. "Nichts" is, we are told, a synonym for the vulgar form "Nix"; but this "Nix" is not what it seems to be, for it involves a pun. On the one hand, "Nix" means 'nothing,' and on the other, 'Nihilum album,' a salve for the eyes made of zinc oxide. Only in certain special circumstances, moreover, does the proverb find application. If one receives "Nichts" as answer to a question, one may

1 Bracton, *De legibus et consuetudinibus Angliae*, IV, xxi, § 4 (Rolls ed., III, 234).

say as repartee, "Nix ist gut für die Augen" ('Nothing is good for the eyes' [but not for me]). This explanation is an old one: Luther must have understood the proverb in somewhat similar fashion, for he says of it, "Minutissima festuca in oculo offendit oculum. Hinc Germani dicunt de remediis oculorum: Nichts ist in die augen gut." In a book devoted to the elucidation rather than the collection of proverbs, *De Oorsprong en Uitlegging van Dagelyks Gebruikte Nederduitsche* (i. e. Dutch) *Spreekwoorden* (Middelburg, 1720), Carolus Tuinman explains *Niet is voor de oogen goed; maar quaad voor de tanden* ('Niet is good for the eyes, but bad for the teeth') by the remark that "niet" is a plant used as a remedy for the eyes. Several signs warn us that this explanation cannot be correct. It disregards the two forms in which the proverb is found: the older with "in die Augen" and the younger with "für die Augen." More than this, it disregards completely the variants, both in German and related languages. The forms *Nothing is good in the eyes, but bad in the stomach (purse, mouth)* are well established in German, Danish, Dutch, Swedish, and no doubt elsewhere. Obviously the proverb is to be understood literally; when its dry humor was no longer effective, the second half of the proverb disappeared and the proverb was used as an empty witticism in repartee without knowledge of its earlier history.

No one of the three explanations of *That's the cheese* commends itself. "One authority suggests that cheese is really the French word 'chose,' and would bid us accept 'C'est la chose' as the true rendering. Another informs us that 'chiz' is Bengalee for 'thing,' and that the expression has been imported from the East; while a third, and he is the man that we [i. e. Hulme] would personally pin our faith on, reminds us that 'choice' was in Anglo-Saxon times 'chese.'"[1] The associations of the phrase link it with colloquial and vulgar speech and give no reason to believe it came from French or Bengalee. Nor are there any signs which suggest that it derives from Old or Middle English: old instances are entirely lacking and there is no such Anglo-Saxon word as Hulme supposes to exist. It is entirely probable that we are dealing with a bit of modern slang.

It is often somewhat difficult to find proverbs which exemplify the retention of archaic forms. Language keeps an old or obsolete word more easily than an old grammatical form. The proverb *When the bale is hest, thenne the bote is nest* contains both words ("bale," 'evil, harm'; "bote," 'remedy') and forms ("hest" for 'highest,' "nest" for 'nearest') which have passed out of use. It is a little difficult to say how long this proverb actually circulated. Perhaps the Elizabethan form *Whan bale is greetest, than is bote a nye-bore* ('neighbor'), which Skeat quotes, may show that the old superlatives had been given up. A more famous example involves changes in the conjugation of the

[1] Hulme, *Proverb Lore*, p. 125.

verb; it is the traditional German rhyme

> Wie die Alten sungen,
> So zwitschern die Jungen
> ('As the old sang,
> So the young twitter'),

which keeps the obsolete verbal form *sungen*. We have similarly an obsolete declensional form in

> Es ist nichts so fein gesponnen,
> Es kommt doch endlich an die Sonnen.

Thus far we have examined chiefly proverbs expressing an ethical truth, in either aphoristic or metaphoric form. There are many sayings which can find no place among such proverbs. Yet the rigid form in which tradition preserves such sayings entitles them to the name proverb. These sayings deal with historical events, legal rights and procedure, the characterization of social or linguistic groups, the weather, health, and certain oft-recurring social situations. Although a metaphor may be used incidentally, it is not of fundamental importance to the saying. These sayings are understood literally.

Historical Proverbs [1]

Proverbs which turn on historical allusions are necessarily rare and short-lived. Since all proverbs make a general application of a particular incident,

1 Ordinarily collections make no distinction between historical and other proverbs. There are special German collections by Wick (*Geographische Ortsnamen, Beinamen und Sprichwörter* [Leipzig, 1896]) and Wurzbach (*Historische Wörter, Sprichwörter und Redensarten* ²[Leipzig, 1866]) and

it is clear that the meaning and implications of the incident must be obvious to speaker and hearer. The handbooks, as well as Heinrich Heine, tell us that *Divide and rule* (Divide et impera) was a maxim of Philip of Macedonia. Polybius, Bossuet, and Montesquieu used it. Others ascribe it to Machiavelli. It was traditionally the motto of Austria. Under such circumstances its unique pertinence to any historical situation would be difficult to demonstrate, although no doubt its origin lies in some particular event. *No grass grows where the Turk's horse has trod* is cited three times between 1639 and 1732, but, as we might expect, it could not maintain itself long after the Turk ceased to threaten Europe. As a rule, the meaning of an historical allusion cannot long remain generally intelligible. Consequently the life of an historical proverb must be very brief, or the allusion must be rendered so general that it no longer has an identifiable connection with the historical fact. This situation appears in a rhyme about James I of England and Queen Anne:

April 23rd, 1619

Queen Ann departed out this life,

King James the first, his loving wife,

Of whom it hath a proverb been,

A hunting King, a dancing Queen.

a special chapter on French historical proverbs in Leroux de Lincy (*Le Livre des Proverbes Français* [2][Paris, 1859]). Ladendorf (*Historisches Schlagwörterbuch* [Strassburg, 1906]) gives few, if any, proverbs, but confines his collection to words and phrases. Compare also W. L. Hertslet, *Treppenwitz der Weltgeschichte* [8] (Berlin, 1912).

The phrase died when it ceased to have meaning and point. The Swedes still figure in German local tradition and story as ravagers, but have left little trace in German proverbs.

The allusion in *No money, no Swiss* (Kein Geld, kein Schweizer) to the service of Swiss mercenaries in European armies may still be intelligible to the general reader, but it is quite beyond our power to attach it to a particular event. If we do so, there is almost no chance of being right. It is, to be sure, customarily assigned to an event in the siege of Milan in 1521, but it would be difficult to prove tradition to be right or wrong. An explanation of *Those who live in glass houses should not throw stones* can be confidently rejected. It has been referred to the so-called Glass House in St. Martin's Fields where the Duke of Buckingham, a favorite of King James I, resided. The Duke supported attacks against the Scotch followers of the king, and in retaliation a crowd smashed the windows of his house. When he complained to the king, the king replied, "Steenie, Steenie, those who live in glass houses should be carfu' how they fling stones." Clearly we have here an allusion to a proverb which was already in existence and not the origin of a proverb. We must of course distinguish between an historical proverb and a proverb which alludes to a custom or condition which no longer exists. *It's good living under the crozier* (Unter dem Krummstab ist gut wohnen) alludes to the preferred situation enjoyed by serfs of ecclesiastical lords, and not to a particular event.

Possibly the proverb *The lucky man takes home* ('marries') *the bride* (Wer Glück hat, führt die Braut heim) has something to do with events of the year 871; but since the proverb is not reported in contemporary accounts of the abduction which is referred to, and since the connection is first suggested by a chronicler seven centuries later, the explanation is more than doubtful. And the explanation that we have here a reminiscence of the "Brautlauf," a foot-race in which the bride was the stake, is equally dubious, although we know this custom existed at Germanic weddings. The proverb probably means only that luck is often the determining factor in success, and not wealth, rank, or cleverness.

A search for historical proverbs is not profitable. In the several books which have been devoted to the subject, we find much material which does not deserve inclusion. The historical allusion is, as we have seen, often uncertain. The phrase may be a scholar's epigram and lack proverbial currency. Most often, perhaps, such collections have erred in including slogans and catch-words of an age, phrases which never passed as proverbs. Such a phrase as *Rum, Romanism, and Rebellion* may enjoy oral and even traditional currency, but it cannot be termed proverbial in any other senses. Seiler quotes *Möck, Mock und Uhl retteten Rottweil* ('Möck, Mock, and Uhl

saved Rottweil') as a Swiss historical proverb, but,
lacking all metaphorical values, it cannot be anything but a schoolmaster's epigram which has perhaps won a longer life than usual.

LEGAL PROVERBS [1]

Although the proverbial evidences of legal customs
and forms are extremely interesting, and although

1 The collection and study of legal proverbs has dealt chiefly with Germanic sources. Little has been done since the publication of the standard German collection by Graf and Dietherr in 1864 (*Deutsche Rechtssprichwörter*), although much is now to be expected from the excellent
introduction of Eberhard, Freiherr von Künssberg, to bibliography and
problems ("Rechtsgeschichte und Volkskunde," *Jahrbuch für Historische Volkskunde* I [1925], 69–125). Introductory bibliographical
materials will be found in Claudius, Freiherr von Schwerin, *Einführung
in das Studium der Germanischen Rechtsgeschichte* (Freiburg i. Br.,
1922), p. 47; D. Martin, *Lawyers' Merriments* (Glasgow, 1912), pp. 47–
59 (hasty, but informative); and the general bibliographies, e. g. Lun-
dell in H. Paul, *Grundriss der Germanischen Philologie*[2], II, i, 1174, for
Scandinavia, and, in general, Bonser, *Proverb Literature* (London, 1930),
pp. 435–439, Nos. 3798–3838.
Important collections and studies devoted to legal proverbs are
chiefly German, e. g. Cohn, *Drei rechtswissenschaftliche Vorträge in
Gemeinverständlicher Darstellung, I, Deutsches Recht im Munde des
Volkes* (Heidelberg, 1888); Eisenhart, *Grundsätze der Deutschen Rechte
in Sprüchwörtern* (Helmstädt, 1759; 2nd ed., Leipzig, 1792; 3rd ed.
by C. E. Otto, Leipzig, 1823); Gierke, *Das Humor im Deutschen Recht*
(Berlin, 1871); Günther, *Recht und Sprache* (Berlin, 1898) and *Deutsche Rechtsaltertümer in unserer Heutigen Sprache* (Leipzig, 1903);
Hillebrand, *Deutsche Rechtssprichwörter* (Zürich, 1858); Koehne, *Gewer-
berechtliches in Deutschen Rechtssprichwörtern* (Zürich, 1915); Rey-
scher, "Die Ueberlieferung der Rechte durch Sprichwörter," *Zeitschrift
für Deutsches Recht und Rechtswissenschaft*, V (1841), 189–209; Winkler,
Deutsches Recht im Spiegel Deutscher Sprichwörter (Leipzig, 1927).
For other languages and countries see Bouthors, *Les Proverbes, Dictons
et Maximes du Droit Rural Traditionnel* (Paris, 1858); Corso, "Kala-
bresische Rechtssprichwörter," *Zeitschrift für Vergleichende Rechts-

there already exists a considerable mass of collection, discussion, and interpretation of these evidences, they have rarely been studied effectively. The apt quotation of a proverb will often turn the course of an argument, just as the apt citation of a precedent may win a case at law. In former days the lower courts before which the peasants appeared used proverbs freely. A German legal document of the fourteenth century declares: "Wherever you can attach a proverb, do so, for the peasants like to judge according to proverbs." [1] The act of quotation recognizes the weight of human experience condensed in the proverb. This weight is necessarily greater than that which any individual's utterance can have. Of course the fundamental defect of proverbial wisdom springs from this same universality. Proverbs are bound to

wissenschaft, XXIII (1910), 289–308; "Proverbi Giuridici Italiani," *Archivio per lo Studio delle Tradizioni Popolari*, XXIII (1907), 484 ff., "Proverbi Giuridici Italiani," *Rivista Italiana di Sociologia*, XX (1916), 581–592, and "Usi Giuridici Contradineschi Ricavate da Massime Popolari," *Circolo Giuridici* (Palermo), XXXIX (1908), 35–48; Saverio, "Collana di Proverbi Giuridici ed Economici Pugliesi," *Rivista Italiana di Sociologia*, XXII (1918), 300–322; Solari, "La Vita Economica nei Proverbi Greci," *ibid.*, II (1898), 187–206, 303–320; Corso, "Proverbi Giuridici Abessini," *ibid.*, XXIV (1920), 150–162; van Hall, *Nieuwe Bijdragen voor Regtsgeleerdheid en Wetgiving*, III (1852), 247–314; A. Corvinus, *Jus Canonicum per Aphorismis* (Amsterdam, 1663); Matthaeus, *Paroemiae Belgarum Jurisconsultis Usitatissimae* (Utrecht, 1667); van Hasselt, *Annotationes ad Antonii Matthaei Paroemias* (1780); Ilu'ustrov, *Iuridičeskiya Poslovitsy i Pogovorki Russkago Naroda* (Moscow, 1885); Koskenjaakko, *Sananlaskututkimuksia, I: Laki* (Helsingfors, 1913).
[1] Quoted by von Künssberg, *Jahrbuch für historische Volkskunde*, I (1925), 72.

the common level of mankind; above it they cannot rise. Yet they display a sound practical sense which even the law itself has not always been able to put into better words: *Better ten guilty escape than one innocent person suffer*; *The extremity of law is the extremity of wrong* (Summum jus, summa injuria); *Right wrongs no man*; *Two wrongs don't make a right*; *Good laws spring from bad morals* (Leges bonae ex malis moribus procreantur).

In Iceland the law-giver, an official of the All-Thing, recited the code annually at the meeting on Thingvellir. The Frisian codes, the first to be written down in any Germanic language, contain metrical or semi-metrical passages in which the form made the work of memory easier. Yet we must not imagine, as some have done,[1] that such codes were highly poetic rhapsodies, "like the recitation of a heroic lay." On the contrary, they employ the language and manner of business, not poetry. The alliterative formulae had the practical purpose of emphasizing and defining legal ideas. They accomplished this by repeating the word or by using one which was more or less nearly synonymous. The latter procedure, the so-called epic variation, is also characteristic of Germanic alliterative verse. The rhythm of these formulae, a natural speech rhythm, is moreover the same as the rhythm

---

[1] R. Koegel, *Geschichte der Deutschen Literatur*, I, 242–259; see further, Siebs, *Zeitschrift für Deutsche Philologie*, XXIX (1897), 405 and "Friesische Literaturgeschichte," in Paul's *Grundriss der Germanischen Philologie*[2], II, i, 527.

of Germanic alliterative verse. But in verse a strict rhythmical regularity and a systematic use of alliteration are required, and, although epic variation is freely employed, the repetition of words is avoided. As we see, alliterative verse and alliterative formulae develop from the same linguistic and rhythmical conditions. The two lines of development are, however, independent, and we must not look upon the formulae as fragments of verse.

Mnemotechnic alliterative formulae [1] which retain the literal words of the law have persisted in common use, and new ones after the same fashion have been invented: *Land und Leute, Haus und Hof, Mann und Maus, hide nor hair, house and home.* We cannot easily distinguish the old from the new in such formulae: *with heart and soul* is Biblical. Not all the old formulae, moreover, are alliterative: *a year and a day* is

---

[1] Typical collections of legal and traditional formulae are Gering (*Zeitschrift für Deutsche Philologie*, XLVIII [1919–20], 304–306 [collected in a review of Feilberg, *Bidrag*]), Willert (*Die Alliterierenden Formeln der Englischen Sprache* [Halle, 1911]), Lean (*Collectanea*, II, 899–940), Heyne (*Formulae Alliterantes ex Antiquis Legibus Frisica Conscriptis Extractae* [Halle, 1884] and "Alliterierende Verse und Reime in den Friesischen Rechtsquellen," *Germania*, IX [1864], 457–499), Koulen (*Der Stabreim im Munde des Volkes zwischen Rhein und Ruhr* [Düren, 1896]), Eiselein (*Die Reimhaften, Anklingenden und Ablautartigen Formeln der Hochdeutschen Sprache* [Leipzig, 1841]), Schulze ("Die sprichwörtlichen Formeln der Deutschen Sprache," *Archiv für das Studium der Neueren Sprachen*, XLVIII [1871], 435–450, XLIX [1872], 139–162, L [1872], 85–122, LI [1873], 195-212, LII [1874], 61–80, 375–392, LIV [1875], 55–74), and Lind ("Rim och verslemningar i de svenska landskapslagarna," *Uppsala Universitets Årsskrift* [1881], No. 3). I have noted only those concerned with Germanic materials. I have not seen Seitz (*Zur Alliteration im Neuenglischen* [Itzehoe, 1883]).

evidently of long standing. Newer formulae are *in any way, shape, or form* (var. *manner*), *to the best of my knowledge and belief*.

Some of these formulae are very interesting. One of the first bits of German lyric verse begins with the formula "Ich bin dein; du bist mein," and, as we might expect, the same words recur constantly in popular love-poetry. But the phrase is more than a mere commonplace: it was part of the wedding ritual. As late as the sixteenth century, Martin Luther knew its use in this connection.

Typical legal proverbs are: *Two words to a bargain*; *Those who will not work shall not eat*; *Root, hog, or die*; *Findings, keepings* (var. *Finders, keepers; losers, weepers*); *Beggars cannot be choosers*; *First come, first served*; *Ein Mann, kein Mann* (i. e. *Testis unus, testis nullus*, 'one witness is no witness.') *My house is my castle* has been declared to be as old as the *Odyssey*, but perhaps not correctly. Curiously enough, parallels do not seem to be very frequent: we may compare the Icelandic *Every man is master at home* (Halr er heima hverr), to which Heusler cites only one parallel, a Gaelic proverb,[1] and the similar and widely known saying *Every cock is proud on his own dunghill*. Sir Edward Coke knew our proverb and puts it: "A man's house is his castle" (Et domus sua est unicuique tutissimum refugium). *Of ill debtours men take oats* means evidently 'Take what you can get in settlement of a bad debt'; oats will do, if wheat is lacking.

1 *Zeitschrift des Vereins für Volkskunde*, XXXV (1915), III, No. 5.

Proverbs which we might scarcely consider as possessing a legal background actually have associations with legal principles. James Howell's important collection of English proverbs (1659) says, for example: "In our Common Law there are some Proverbs that carry a kind of authority with them, as that which began in Henry the Fourth's time, He that bulls the cow must keep the calf." The reference is, of course, to an illegitimate child. In contrary fashion, the legal allusion may be entirely different from what it superficially appears to be: *Necessity knows no law* probably refers, not to necessity in a general sense, but to necessity forced upon one by the need of self-defence. In other words, *Necessity knows no law* means 'in defending one's self all means are legal.' It was in this special legal sense, of course, that the proverb was used by the German chancellor, von Bethmann-Hollweg, in his speech before the Reichstag in defence of the invasion of Belgium.

Certain fields are richly represented in legal proverbs: notably rights in real and personal property, e. g. *Suum cuique*, a venerable saying; the bases on which claims for privileges and consideration may rest; the rules of testimony. Proverbs connected with the handicrafts are relatively abundant, while those associated with mercantile pursuits are less frequent. Legal proverbs dealing with mercantile affairs are ordinarily concerned with the rights of buyer and seller and therefore touch the interests of the common

man closely: *Caveat emptor* ('Let the buyer beware')
— compare the German *Augen auf, Kauf ist Kauf*
('Keep your eyes open; a sale is a sale') — is an ancient warning.[1]

Often the legal principle involved in proverbs is
still valid; e. g. *No receiver, no thief; The hailer* ('receiver') *is as bad as the stailer* ('thief'); *Better steal a
horse than stand by and look on* exemplify the legal
principle that aiding and abetting a thief renders
one equally guilty with him. In the oldest form of
The hailer is as bad as the stailer, the assertion is
general and concerns the accessory to any crime.
Later it is restricted, as in the preceding instances, to
thievery or is altered into the assertion, which accords
with mediaeval legal practice, that the accessory after
the fact is more guilty than the criminal. Other legal
proverbs refer to punishments no longer employed,
e. g. *Mitgefangen, mitgehangen* ('Caught with [a crim-
inal], hanged with [a criminal]') or the variant *Mit-
gegangen, mitgefangen, mitgehangen* ('Those who have
accompanied and have been caught with [thieves] are
hanged with them'). So severe a punishment for
theft (if, as is probable, theft is meant) points to a
considerable age for this proverb, and the same is true
of *As well be hanged for a sheep as a lamb*. The Ger-

---

1 See the Latin proverbs on business and money collected by Otto,
"Geldverkehr und Besitz im [Lateinischen] Sprichwort," *Archiv für
Lateinische Lexikographie*, VI (1889), 47–58, and p. 15 above. See an
interesting small collection of German proverbs in a merchant's hand-
book: P. J. Marperger, *Nothwendig und Nützliche Fragen über die
Kaufmannschaft* (Leipzig, 1714), pp. 429–446.

mans in Bohemia now say *Mitgehanga, mitgefanga* and explain it as meaning 'He who participates ("mitgehanga") is called to account with the actual criminal,' but in so doing they have exchanged the meanings of the two words in the proverb. *Service is no heritage* alludes to feudal customs, and has necessarily passed out of use. Similarly *The king can do no wrong* is no longer accepted as true. Some legal proverbs have died even though the idea expressed by them persists: Chaucer said "Promise is dette," which, although now lost, is paralleled by *His word is as good as his bond.*

Many legal proverbs are ultimately Latin in origin: *Ignorance of the law excuses no one*; *Silence gives consent* (Qui tacet, consentire videtur); *Ein Wort, kein Wort* ('One word is naught') or *Ein Mann, kein Mann* (Testis unus, testis nullus).

Those legal proverbs which describe a situation or indicate a course of action which can scarcely ever have been legally justified form an especially interesting group. Such proverbs are *All's fair in love and war*; *A fair exchange is no robbery*; *Einen Kuss in Ehren kann niemand wehren* ('No one can object to an honorable kiss'). Some of these can be explained by reference to the historical background from which the saying sprang or by study of the variants. For example, the obvious literal interpretation of *A fair exchange is no robbery* is of course out of the question legally, until we understand that it refers to an exchange effected by force by a person in flight. In order to disguise himself a man can exchange clothing and such a forcible exchange is not reckoned as theft. *Einen Kuss in Ehren kann niemand wehren* has been declared to be a quotation from the German Anacreontic poet, Hölty; but it was in print before he was born. Our conceptions have changed regarding the ideas expressed in some proverbs: *Bis an't kni is't fri* ('Up to the knee is permitted') is a Low German proverb alluding to the degree of liberty permitted.

As in any proverb, the allusion in a legal proverb may be obscure and call for explanation. Perhaps *Possession is nine points of the law* or the older form *Possession is eleven points of the law* refers merely to the ten or dozen conceived of as a unit; in that case we need not seek to discover what the points really are.

A very important class of legal proverbs finds comparatively little use today, although it once constituted a significant part of legal practice. The gist of the law was condensed into maxims which circulated in legal groups, were collected in handbooks, and found a place in pleading and even judicial decisions. In modern times we have something similar in G. Cohn, *Das Neue Deutsche Bürgerliche Recht in Sprüchen* (Berlin, 1896–1900), which turns the German code into brief and easily remembered sentences. For the most part, popular tradition was unable to take up and preserve the mediaeval legal maxims because the precision of their Latin form did not readily per-

mit of translation and because the distinctions involved did not obviously and immediately concern
common folk. Yet we must regard these maxims as
proverbs, although of a very special kind, for they are
anonymous, traditional, and epigrammatic. Every
calling in which the practitioners use freely a body
of relatively esoteric information is likely to possess
such professional maxims. Typical examples of legal
maxims are *Ultra posse nemo obligatur* ('No one is
bound beyond his power') and the variant *Impossi-
bilium nulla obligatio est* ('The impossible is no obligation'), *Socii mei socius meus socius non est* ('The
companion of my companion is not my companion'),
Res judicata pro veritate accipitur ('Things adjudi-
cated are considered true'), *Quod initio vitiosum est
non potest tractu temporis convalescere* ('What is wrong
in its beginnings cannot be remedied by the passage
of time'), *Domus sua cuique est tutissimum refugium*
('A man's house is his safest refuge', *An Englishman's
house is his castle*), *Cessante ratione legis cessat ipsa
lex* ('When the reason for the law no longer exists, the
law ceases to exist'), *Volenti non fit injuria* ('No in-
jury is done to one who is willing'). The examples
cited thus far can be traced back to the great body of
Roman law and its commentators. A few which have
been quoted have established themselves in popular
tradition; others of the same kind are *Ignorance of the
law excuses no one*; *Silence gives consent*. Occasionally
we find maxims which appear to be modifications of

the Roman law or to represent separate English developments: *De minimis non curat lex* ('The law does
not concern itself with minor matters'); *Qui facit per
alium facit per se* ('He who commits an act by another's agency commits the act himself'); but in such
matters we are touching on difficult points in legal
history. The origin and use of these maxims is little
studied; the best introduction to them, a brief essay
by James Williams, concludes in part as follows:
"Few students of jurisprudence would be qualified,
and probably still fewer would be willing, to devote
the time to a careful search among the voluminous
and forgotten writings of jurists whose very names are
only known to students of the history of the law." [1]

A considerable body of popular law has never crys-
tallized in formulae, and although it is extremely interesting and little known it cannot be examined here.
Such legal superstitions, if we may call them so, are:
witnesses cannot testify to what is seen through glass
(although this belief does not seem to exclude the
wearer of spectacles), pregnant women cannot testify,
a blow struck against a man wearing glasses is subject
to severer punishment than another kind of assault.
The collection and study of such notions deserve to be
undertaken, but they do not in the main find expres-

[1] "Latin Maxims in English Law," *The Law Magazine and Law Review*,
4th Ser., XX (1895), 283–295. See a small collection of such maxims
in J. Michelet, *Les Origines du Droit* (Paris,1837), p. lxxiii, note, and
L. Volkmar, *Paroemia et Regulae Juris Romanorum, Germanorum,
Franco-Gallorum, Britannorum* (Berlin, 1854).

sion in legal proverbs. Possibly we may see allied material in such proverbs as *Don't hit* (var. *kick*) *a man when he is down*; *A taleteller is worse than a thief*; *Among friends all things are common*, which is an idea perhaps to be traced back to the Pythagorean society; *Hands off is fair play*.

"BLASON POPULAIRE" [1]

Men are always ready to mock their neighbors, and from time immemorial witticisms have passed be-

1 Miscellaneous bibliographical notes will be found in Gaidoz and Sébillot (*Blason Populaire de la France* [Paris, 1884] and the *Catalogus van Folklore*['s Gravenhage, 1919–1922]). The best collections are French. Unfortunately there is no good discussion of the problems in the field of local witticisms; after Schulte ("Spottnamen und -verse auf Ortschaften im nördlichen Oberhessen," *Hessische Blätter für Volkskunde*, IV [1905], 142–167) the best introductions are the prefaces to the collections, notably Dejardin (*Dictionnaire des Spots ou Proverbes Wallons* [Liège, 1863, 2d ed., 1891]). Typical collections are Lean (*Collectanea*, I, 11–343), who gives English and Italian materials; Dejardin, as above; Raadt (*Les Sobriquets des Communes Belges* [Brussels, 1903]); Gittée ("Steden en Dorpen tegen Elkander," *Volkskunde* [Ghent], V [1892], 124–138, 167–179); Barjavel (*Dictons et Sobriquets Patois des Villes . . . du Département de Vaucluse* [Carpentras, 1849]); Canel (*Blason Populaire de la Normandie* [Caen, 1859]); Gaidoz and Sébillot, as above; O. de Watteville (*Etude sur les Devises Personnelles* [Paris, 1888]); A. Ledieu (*Blason Populaire de la Picardie* [Paris, 1905]); Handelmann (*Topographischer Volkshumor* [Kiel, 1886]); Hesekiel (*Land und Stadt im Volksmunde* [Berlin, 1867]); Schlauch (*Sachsen im Sprichwort* [Leipzig, 1905]); Wick (*Geographische Ortsnamen, Beinamen und Sprichwörter* [Leipzig, 1896]); Cornelissen (*Nederlandsche Volkshumor* [Antwerp, n.d.]); Goebel (*De Graecarum Civitatum Proprietatibus Proverbio Notatis* [Breslau, 1915]). Examples of older, related collections are Caviceo (*Urbium Dicta ad Maximilianum Primum Romanorum Regem* [Parma, 1491]) and Ritio (*Le Nomi et Cognomi*, etc. [1585], reprinted in *Due Opuscoli Rarissimi del Secolo XVI* [Scelta di curiosità letterarie, XCII, Bologna, 1865]).

tween man and man, village and village, country and
country. A word or a pointed phrase singles out a
characteristic trait which seems to be hereditary or at
least dominant — the presence or, more frequently,
the absence of a quality. Physical peculiarities, the
dark hair of southern peoples or the light hair and
blue eyes of northern Germany, are rarely commented
on. Stupidity, greed, miserliness, and such antisocial
qualities are favored subjects. Ordinarily the hearer
perceives readily enough the barb in the remark, for
the wit is rarely subtle. The attitude is sufficiently
illustrated by Nathanael's remark to Philip: "Can
there any good thing come out of Nazareth?" (A
Nazareth potest aliquid boni esse? *John* i, 46), but we
cannot be sure of the proverbial currency of this allusion. Tacitus (*Ann.*, xiv, 7) tells us that the murder-
ous affray in which the inhabitants of Pompeii and
Nuceria engaged in the days of Nero took rise in
mutual raillery. Although the insults are no longer
preserved, we need have little doubt regarding their
general nature and intent.

The characterization of races and nations is found
both in single descriptive words, *frog-eater, square-
head, boche*, and in proverbial sayings. With the former we are not particularly concerned, although it is
well-nigh certain that curious facts regarding them
can be discovered by the careful searcher.[1] Perhaps,

1 See, for example, T. Roth, *Völkernamen in ihrer Entwicklung zu Gat-
tungsnamen*, Friedland i. M., 1909-10; M. Spiegel, *Völkernamen als*

for example, it might be shown that French racial and provincial names are often derived from references to food and eating, while this is less true of other countries. Nor need we linger over the very definite associations which have in many cases attached themselves to certain places. Villages and groups of people have distinguished themselves for their folly, like the three wise men of Gotham. Every country has its Abdera or its Schilda.¹ Bœotia has an immortality of a sort, along with Sybaris and Miletus. The poverty of a village seems to become proverbial more often than its wealth.² With such traditional characterizations we might compare the Irishman, Scotchman, or Yankee of stage and story.

The brief characterizations of a neighboring village or people which the French call "blason populaire" and the German "Ortsneckereien," and for which there is no convenient English term, are truly popular. Some are merely traditional insults which have lost all meaning in the course of time. The Greeks and later the Romans said that the Cretans were liars (*Mendax Creta*). The word "Erbfeind," 'hereditary enemy,' which I suppose everyone now thinks alludes to France, once meant the Devil (and is comparable

Epitheta im Gallo-romanischen (extract of a dissertation [Berlin, 1921]); F. Boillot, *Répertoire des Métaphores Français tirés des Noms des Villes et des Pays Étrangers* (Paris, 1929).

1 See a very useful list in Gaidoz-Sébillot, *Blason Populaire*, p. vi, and Schulte's collection for the different provinces of Germany in *Hessische Blätter für Volkskunde*, IV (1905), 146.

2 Schulte, as above, pp. 151–153.

in English to the Arch Enemy) and later the Turk.
The Italians say of the French:

> Tutto fanno, niente sanno,
> Niente sanno, tutto fanno.

> ('They do everything, they know nothing,
> They know nothing, they do everything').

Perhaps most such local nicknames contain a hostile or at least an unfriendly suggestion. There are, however, a few sayings which are simply descriptive; of these the most famous is no doubt *Frisia non cantat* ('Frisia does not sing'). There are, furthermore, some sayings which seem to be the direct opposite in spirit of these local nicknames: one admirable trait is singled out as characteristic. Probably such phrases were invented by the group itself rather than by its neighbors. Typical examples are *Deutsche Treue*; *La belle France*; *Merry England*.

Epigrammatic characterizations of several peoples are frequent enough, particularly in the Romance languages. A typical example is

> Ingles borracho,
> Frances gabacho,
> Hollandes mantequero,
> Español gran caballero.

> ('The Englishman a drunkard,
> The Frenchman a scoundrel,
> The Dutchman a farmer,
> The Spaniard a gentleman.')

The epigram is interesting for the indication which it gives of the age in which it was invented, an age when Spain was in contact with England, France, and the Netherlands. German examples are rare, but the following characterization of four Hessian villages shows that the form is not entirely unknown:

> Niederohme — Dreacksome,
> Habach — hatt Kartoffelsaat,
> Ermerod — der Bär brummt,
> Elperod — die Kaffeestadt.

In explanation we are told that Niederohmen supplied the adjoining territory with flax seed and Habach with seed potatoes; in Ermenrod a peasant once mistook an ass for a bear and called for help, saying, "The bear is growling"; and Elpenrod was the center for coffee and sugar. Such a characterization is not particularly interesting. The examples which are definitely associated with the Romance languages have found a wider dissemination than such local rhymes ever could. The saying *The Jews spend their money at the Feast of the Passover; the Moors, at weddings; and the Christians, in law-suits* is asserted to be originally Spanish, and even more widely known is *The Italian is wise before the deed; the German, in the deed; and the Frenchman, after the deed.* Such a characterization as *England is the paradise of women, hell of horses, and purgatory of servants* is certainly not of English make. The spirit of the Reformation is abundantly apparent in an epigram which is quite probably German in invention: *A Polish bridge, a Bohemian monk, a Swabian nun, an Austrian soldier, Italian reverence, and German fasting are worth a bean* (Pons Polonicus: monachus Boemicus: Suevica monialis: miles Australis: Italorum devotio et Alemannorum ieiunia: fabam valent omnia). It is difficult to know to what extent such epigrams were popular. Many, I suspect, are no more than semi-literary witticisms which enjoyed only a short life.

In longer characterizations, which may now and again be termed proverbial, we recognize many which attempt more or less successfully to name essential or typical merits of various countries. *Italia para nacer, Francia para vivir, España para morir* praises the climate of Italy, the gaiety of France, and the piety of Spain. After the Renaissance, such group characterizations appear to have enjoyed great popularity and to have been translated from one language into another. It is rather doubtful whether many such sayings ever became firmly established among the folk. We know little or nothing about their origin, history, or stylistic peculiarities. A few of these epigrams may well be of local origin, perhaps even without the suggestion of foreign models, e. g. *Cheshire for men, Berkshire for dogs, Bedfordshire for naked flesh, and Lincolnshire for bogs*; and the previously cited German quatrain.

We do not know exactly how these longer epigrams were composed. Apparently certain single characterizations were capable of being transferred from one epigram to another, and perhaps the fashion was transmitted in this way. The power of Venice, for example, appears in more than one connection during the fifteenth and sixteenth centuries. An early mention is in a description of the Italian cities ascribed to Messer Pandolfo Collenuctio, ambassador of Gostanzo Sforza: *Auctoritas pontificis, sapientia regis* (sc. Neapolis), *potentia venetorum, arma mediolanensium, aurum florentinorum* ('The authority of the Pope, the wisdom of the king [of Naples], the power of the Venetians, the arms of the Milanese, the gold of the Florentines'). Such an epigram has a unity arising from the fact that only Italian cities are mentioned. In the next century there is an analogous German saying:

> Nürnberger Witz,
> Strassburger Geschütz,
> Venetier Macht,
> Augsburger Pracht,
> Ulmer Geld,
> Wer dieses hätte, wäre reich in dieser Welt.

('The wit of Nuremberg, the artillery of Strassburg, the power of Venice, the splendor of Augsburg, the money of Ulm: whoever had this would be rich in this world').

The presence in the German epigram of the allusion to Venice suggests very strongly that it was modelled directly or indirectly on the Italian one.[1]

[1] A long list of feminine charms, ranging in number from seven to thirty, has been handed down by literary tradition rather than by word of

The traditional mockery of certain trades offers many interesting problems, for we do not always clearly understand why some trades should be the object of scorn and suspicion and others go unscathed. Why, for example, should the tailor be a conventional object of ridicule and the cobbler rarely? We also know very little about the variations from country to country; different trades are mocked in different countries, and even when the same trade is being held up to ridicule, different formulae and different associations are employed. The material at our disposal for the study of such problems is comparatively abundant and reliable, but very little has been accomplished as yet.[1] Often a readily intelligible attitude of the peasant is reflected in these sayings. The peasant who deals with the miller doubts the miller's

mouth. Although the occurrences are numerous, their relations have never been studied fully. Since the list is scarcely proverbial, I cannot discuss it here. See Haltaus, *Liederbuch der Clara Hätzlerin* (Bibliothek der Gesamten Deutschen National-Literatur, VIII [Quedlinburg, 1840]), p. lxviii; R. Koehler, *Kleinere Schriften* (ed. J. Bolte), III (Weimar, 1900), 31 ff.; Küffner, *Die Deutschen im Sprichwort*, pp. 200, 253*a–c*; Wesselski, *Angelo Polizianos Tagebuch* (Jena, 1929), p. 93, No. 195.

[1] Albrecht Keller, *Die Handwerker im Volkshumor* (Leipzig, 1912); P. Sébillot, *Légendes et Curiosités des Métiers* (Paris, 1895); H. F. Feilberg, *Bidrag til en Jysk Ordbog* (Copenhagen, 1886–1914); H. Klenz, *Schelten-Wörterbuch* (Strassburg, 1910). L. Ricker (*Zur landschaftlichen Synonomik der Deutschen Handwerkernamen* [Freiburg i. Br., 1917]) gives nicknames for the potter, cooper, and cabinet-maker. In an admirable article, which is soon to appear, Barbara Salditt traces the origin and dissemination of the traditional association of the tailor and the goat; see "Der Schneider und die Geiss im Deutschen Volksmunde bis zum siebzehnten Jahrhundert," *Hessische Blätter für Volkskunde*, XXX (1931).

honesty in taking toll for the grinding of grain: *The miller has a golden thumb*. Similarly the tailor is accused of cutting cloth to his own advantage: *The tailor cuts three sleeves for every woman's gown*. Equally curious and interesting are those traditional associations which do not spring from the obvious relations of the peasant to the trade, but these associations do not in general take proverbial form. We find cowardice mentioned as a typical trait of the tailor: *It takes nine tailors to make a man*. Other traditional slurs do not appear as proverbs: the association of the tailor and the goat, which is restricted to Germany, has left no record in proverbs. The origin and history of these traditional insults are often interesting problems in the history of culture.

Many traditional sayings show a keen recognition of linguistic resemblances or peculiarities. So far as I have observed, they seem to be more abundant in German than in English. Characteristic similarities between English and the Frisian language spoken on the islands along the coast of the Netherlands, Germany, and Denmark and on the adjoining mainland appear in *Eggs, butter, and cheese are good English and good Freese* and *Gooid brade, botter, and sheese is good Halifax and good Freese*. The rhyme

> Nä, nich und jawol
> is Brôkmer Prôtcoll.
> Nee, neet un jawall
> Seggen de Krummhörners all

indicates certain distinctive peculiarities of the Frisian dialects on the northwest coast of Germany in the vicinity of Emden. The Low German saying *In Friesland one eats Brugge* ('bridges,' 'butter cakes'), *walks on Mühlen* ('mills,' 'slippers'), *and keeps Schaipen* ('sheep,' 'coins worth about ten cents') *in a bag* involves a pun in each of the significant words: the first meaning is Low German and the second Frisian. There is a curious instance in which the explanation does not make the situation clear: we are told that the Swabian proverb *A Swabian has no heart but two Magen* (Ein Schwabe hat kein Herz aber zwei Magen ['stomachs']) rests upon the supposedly Swabian dialectal peculiarity of using *Magen* for *Herz*. Inasmuch as this peculiarity is not registered in the large Swabian dialect dictionary and the same proverb is, furthermore, used of Prussians, the explanation is rather dubious. An English proverb which concerns itself with the peculiarities of local speech is *By Tre, Pol, and Pen, you shall know the Cornish men*, which refers to three words, 'town,' 'head,' and 'top' respectively, frequently found in Cornish place-names and proper names. Those who live in the town of Glarus mock their neighbors with the traditional sentence "Hæidər odər wæidər odər hæidr šu kxæ?" i. e. 'Habt ihr oder wollt ihr oder habt ihr schon gehabt?' [1] This sentence illustrates two striking details in which

1 C. Streiff, *Die Laute der Glarner Mundarten* (Beiträge zur Schweizerdeutschen Grammatik, VIII [Frauenfeld, 1915]), p. 36, § 44. So also in Winteler, *Die Kerenzer Mundart* (Leipzig, 1876), p. 192, No. 1.

the neighboring dialects differ from that of Glarus. In Glarus "habt" (hæid) and "wollt" (wænd) cannot possibly rhyme, while in the dialects illustrated by the sentence the rhyme is perfect. The form "kxæ" (gehabt) differs very considerably from that found in Glarus and most Swiss dialects. Obviously we cannot always know when the traditional phrase merely illustrates the linguistic peculiarities of a group and when it serves to mock one's neighbors.

For various regions of Germany we have distinctive traditional sentences of rhymes which indicate characteristic dialectal traits: *Eine jute jebratene Jans ist eine jute Jabe Jottes* exemplifies the spirant [j] for [g] of Berlin speech; *Der Riese Ragi auf dem Rathaus zu Bremen* and *Reiner Roggen, Bremer Brot*, the typical guttural [r] of Bremen; *Es heisst nicht hēst, es hēst heisst*, the pronounciation of [ai] as [ē] in Dresden; and *Anna sass auf einem spitzen Stein*, the Hanoverian [sp] and [st] for [šp] and [št] of standard German. *Heute trägt der Heide Häute über die Heide* plays with Saxon dialectal traits, for "heute," "Heide," and "Häute" are usually pronounced differently. The Norwegian *Boner spiser Böner* ('Peasants eat beans') involves an essential distinction between simple and compound accent. The most famous instance in which a dialectal trait was utilized is recounted as follows: "And the Gileadites took the passages of Jordan before the Ephraimites: and it was so, that when those Ephraimites which were escaped, said,

Let me go over; that the men of Gilead said unto him, Art thou an Ephraimite? If he said, Nay, then said they unto him, Say now 'Shibboleth'; and he said 'Sibboleth': for he could not frame to pronounce it right. Then they took him, and slew him at the passages of the Jordan." (Judges xii, 5–6.) From this incident we have of course the proverbial use of *shibboleth*.

Although we cannot distinguish sharply these various classes of proverbial linguistic observations, there is another group which includes combinations of words difficult to pronounce. Some such combinations contain difficult and characteristic sounds and combinations like the Polish *Chrząszcz brzmi w trzcinie* [xšoⁿšč bžmⁱi f tščⁱinⁱe], i. e. 'Beetle buzzes in reeds,' or the Bohemian *Strč brk skrz krk a krk skrz brk*, i. e. 'Stick a quill through [your] throat and a throat through the quill,' and *Tři a třicet stříbrných křepelek přeskočili tři a třicet stříbrných střech*, i. e. 'Thirty-three silver quails jumped over thirty-three silver roofs.' These sentences illustrate the typical sibilants and the Bohemian syllabic *r*. The English "tongue-twisters," e. g. *Peter Piper picked a peck of pickled peppers*; *She sells sea-shells by the seashore*; *Bill had a billboard and also a board bill, but the board bill bored Bill so that he sold the billboard to pay the board bill*, belong to the more usual type of such phrases. As we see, they do not concern themselves with characteristic and unusual sounds in English speech, for *w*, *th* in "there," and *th* in "thin" are not mentioned. Sentences of this sort are ordinarily composed of sounds which a child finds it difficult to form and not of sounds peculiar to a particular language. In general, linguistic proverbs, shibboleths, and "tongue-twisters" are concerned with consonants rather than vowels, although Finnish, a language in which vowel quantity is all-important, has some sentences involving vowels.

WEATHER PROVERBS [1]

It is of course difficult to separate proverbs about the weather from superstitions and traditions which

1 In addition to the bibliographies in most collections of weather proverbs, e.g. Inwards, *Weather Lore* (London, 1893), there are admirable lists in *Schweizer Volkskunde*, XIV (1924), 16 and Bonser, *Proverb Literature* (London, 1930), pp. 422–429, Nos. 3675–3746. The following collections are important. England and America: Dunwoody, *Weather Proverbs*, Signal Service Notes IX (Washington, 1883); Humphreys, *Weather Proverbs and Parodoxes* (Baltimore, 1923); Inwards, as above; Swainson, *A Handbook of Weather Folk-lore* (London, 1873). France: Corbis, "Recueil des Dictons Populaires sur le Temps," *Bulletin de la Société Belfortaine d'Emulation*, VIII (1886–87), 19–30; XIV (1895), 109–115; F. de Roucy, *Dictons Populaires sur le Temps* (Paris, 1878). Germany: Bahlmann, *Alt-Münsterische Bauern-Reime* (Münster, 1896); Haldy, *Die Deutschen Bauernregeln* (Jena, 1923), a recent popular collection without notes; Müldener, *Das Buch vom Wetter oder das Wetter im Sprichwort* (Bernburg, n. d.); Reinsberg-Düringsfeld, *Das Wetter im Sprichwort* (Leipzig, 1864); Walter, *Wettersprüche* (Braunschweig, 1920); Wimmert, "Bauern- und Wetterregeln aus dem Rheinlande," *Zeitschrift für Deutsche Mundarten*, 1910, pp. 351–356. The Netherlands: van Hall, *Spreekwoorden en Voorschriften in Spreuken Betreffend Landbouw en Weêrkennis* (Haarlem, 1872); Thijm, *Kalender- en Gezondheidsregels* (Uitgaven der Koninklijke Vlaamsche Akademie, III, 9 [Ghent, 1893]); Beets, "Volkswijsheid over het Weer," *Verslagen en Mededeelingen van het Vlaamsche*

are definite in substance but not in form. The advice
"Don't plant corn until the dogwood is in bloom,"
which is current in eastern Pennsylvania and perhaps
elsewhere, has not received final form as a proverb,
nor has the widespread superstition regarding the
groundhog and his shadow. Many such sayings, furthermore, do not involve a forecast of weather; consequently Frick, who has written extensively on the
style and construction of weather proverbs, excludes
them from consideration. Proverbs which contain no
forecast tell when certain migratory birds arrive or
leave:

> The cuckoo comes in April,
> Sings a song in May;
> Then in June another tune,
> And then she flies away

or

> The first cock of hay
> Frights the cuckoo away;

Akademie, XXI (1908), 553–592 (an essay which is little more than a
paraphrase of Yermoloff). Portugal: Thomaz Pires, *Calendario Rural*
(Elvas, 1898). Russia: Yermoloff, *Die Landwirtschaftliche Volksweisheit
in Sprichwörtern, Redensarten und Wetteregeln*, I (Leipzig, 1905). Spain:
Rodríguez Marín, *Cien Refranes Andaluces de Meteorología, Cronología,
Agricultura y Economía Rural* [2] (Seville, 1894) and *Los Refranes del
Almanaque* (Seville, 1896). Sweden: Hildebrandsson, "Samling af Be-
märkelsedagar, Tecken, Märken, Ordspråk och Skrock Rörande Väder-
leken," *Antikvarisk Tidskrift för Sverige*, VII, pt. 2 (1883), 1–106.
Switzerland: Seelig, *Die Jahreszeiten im Spiegel Schweizerischer Volks-
sprüche* (Zürich, 1925). Most studies of weather proverbs deal with
their meteorological aspects. The most significant studies are by Frick
("Le Peuple et la Prévision du Temps," *Schweizerisches Archiv für
Volkskunde*, XXVI [1926], 1–21, 89–100, 171–188, 254–279); Hellmann,
"Uber den Ursprung der Volkstümlichen Wetterregeln (Bauernre-
geln)," *Sitzungsberichte der Preussischen Akademie, Physikalisch-
Mathematische Klasse* (1923), 148–170; and Yermoloff, as above.

what weather characterizes certain months (*March comes in like a lion and goes out like a lamb*);[1] when crops should be planted; how the days grow longer or shorter; or what hygienic precautions are necessary at certain seasons:

> When the wind is in the east,
> It is good for neither man nor beast.

All these sayings and the weather proverbs which involve a forecast differ in a significant matter from ordinary proverbs: they contain no metaphorical shift of meaning. A weather proverb of whatever kind means what it says and no more. Of course there are proverbs taken from weather conditions which employ a metaphor, e. g. *Every cloud has a silver lining*; *The darkest hour is just before dawn*; *It never rains but it pours*, but these cannot properly pass as weather proverbs.

Many traditional forecasts of weather conditions can be called truly proverbial: *April showers bring May flowers*; *Rain before seven stops before eleven*;

> Mackerel sky, mackerel sky,
> Never long wet, never long dry.

1 The longer form of this proverb,

> March hack ham ('black ram')
> Comes in like a lion,
> Goes out like a lamb,

is clearly derived from verses in a calendar. The obscure reference to Aries, the ram, in the zodiac has been lost in later forms. Today, the proverb is perhaps more often regarded as a prophecy: "*If* March comes in like a lion, it goes out like a lamb."

As the days begin to lengthen,
The cold begins to strengthen.

It is interesting to note that the old rhyme

Evening red and morning gray
Will speed a traveler on his way;
But evening gray and morning red
Will pour down rain upon his head

appears, perhaps for the first time, in the New Testament: "When it is evening, ye say, It will be fair weather: for the sky is red. And in the morning, It will be foul weather today: for the sky is red and lowring" (*Matt.* xvi, 2–3). Occasionally a proverb bears within itself an indication of the circumstances under which it arose:

A rainbow at night
Is the sailor's (*var.* fisher's, shepherd's) delight;
A rainbow in the morning
Is the sailor's (*var.* fisher's, shepherd's) warning.

On the whole, weather proverbs which clearly belong to the sea and sailors are surprisingly few; perhaps the manner in which our collections of proverbs have been made has hindered their discovery and preservation. The few classical Greek instances of weather proverbs are, as Hellmann [1] points out, typically concerned with the winds and the sea and in this way reflect the sea-faring life of their inventors.

1 Hellmann, *Sitzungsberichte der Preussischen Akademie, Physikalisch-Mathematische Klasse,* 1923, p. 159.

Most weather proverbs refer to certain signs which are believed to forecast the weather. They mark the beginning of spring by the appearance of migratory birds or the growth of characteristic plants. Others give directions about the planting of crops or foretell the weather of certain later weeks or months from the weather on certain days. If they are taken in a sufficiently general sense, some truth may ordinarily be found in them — but then the observation is so readily apparent or conveys so little of a definite sort that it has small value in the meteorologist's eyes. Even the weather proverbs themselves suggest that the speaker did not take his own words too seriously:

> Wenn der Hahn kräht auf dem Mist,
> Wird's anders oder es bleibt wie's ist.

> ('When the cock crows on the dunghill,
> The weather will change or it will stay as it is'.)

The doubt here expressed is no new trait in weather proverbs: in a manuscript of the fourteenth or fifteenth century in the Brunswick city library we read

> Si pluit in festo processi martiniani
> Quadriginta dies continuare solet
> Hoc intelige sic si non pluit hic pluit illic.

('If it rains during the feast of the procession of St. Martinianus, it usually continues for forty days. Understand it thus: if it does not rain here, it rains there'.)[1]

All signs fail in dry weather expresses a similar idea of the value of popular weather forecasts.

1 Hellmann, as above, p. 152. I have expanded abbreviations.

We distinguish proverbs which deal solely with crops, storms, and fair weather at sea, and forecasts of the weather from natural signs, from proverbs in which the days of the calendar play a part. Hellmann, who writes learnedly on the origin of weather proverbs, believes that proverbs of the more general sort in which the calendar is not mentioned are perhaps ultimately classical in their beginnings, although he is able to cite only one Latin instance, a parallel to *April showers bring May flowers*, and a few Greek instances of a very special kind concerned with the winds and the sea. In the *Saturnalia* (v, 20, 18) Macrobius preserves for us this Latin example, "an old rustic saw" (rusticum vetus canticum): "Hiberno pulvere verno luto grandia farra, Camille, metes" ('With winter dust and spring mud you will reap, Camillus, big harvests'), which we may compare to the English *A bushel* (var. *peck*) *of March dust is worth a king's ransom*. A characteristic trait which appears in this and many other weather proverbs is the description of the weather in terms of its effects: "winter dust" instead of "drought." Perhaps we may conclude with Hellmann that Macrobius' saying belongs to dry central Italy rather than to lower Italy or Sicily, where a more definite rainy season prevails.

Proverbs in which reference is made to the calendar — and ordinarily to specific days — must have originated at a time when knowledge of the calendar was common property. They cannot be extremely old, for the general use of any form of calendar indicating the separate days dates only from the late Middle Ages. The peasant still thinks in terms of Lammastide and St. Martin's Day rather than those of our calendar. In such proverbs a remarkable agreement over a wide area can often be observed, and not infrequently we can see that the proverb has been carried to a region where it is quite out of place. An adaptation to different climates appears in the English *March grass never did good* and the Norwegian *April's growth is rarely good* (Aprils grode er sjelden til gode).[1]

The inapplicability of weather proverbs in regions to which they have been carried by cultural currents appears in meteorological matters. Hellmann, for example, believes that *A green Christmas, a white Easter*, which is widely known in all the Western European languages, must have arisen in a region where snow ordinarily lies on the ground at Christmas. It cannot be native to regions where the ground is bare at Christmas, since snow at Easter is unusual in most parts of Europe. Probably this argument is correct. Nevertheless, it is hard to understand why the proverb is so widely disseminated in the Romance languages, spoken in countries where the meteorological conditions are even more unfavorable than in Germany. It may be that the proverb was invented in a region where snow is usual at Christmas; and its

[1] Kock and Petersen, *Ostnordiska och Latinska Medeltidsordsprå k* (Copenhagen, 1889–94), II, 88.

persistence may be ascribed to contrast, both in form
and substance: undue warm weather will be balanced
by cold.

In weather proverbs which mention a particular
day in the calendar, a conflict between the facts and
the day named may make it possible to assign an ap-
proximate age to the tradition. For example, English,
French, and German proverbs connect St. Barnabas'
Day (June 11) with the summer solstice, e. g. *Barnaby
bright, the longest day and the shortest night*. Clearly this
refers to dates in "old style" and enables us to fix the
origin of the proverb in the fifteenth century, when
the calendar was about ten days behind the true time.
In the same way *Lucy Light, the shortest day and
the longest night*, which is a companion in form to
the proverb just quoted, and the German saying
St. Lucy's (December 13) *makes the days stop getting
shorter* (Sankt Luzen macht den Tag stutzen) refer to
the winter solstice and must have originated about
A.D. 1350, when the Julian calendar was eight days
behind. Before the calendar was changed on the continent, i. e. before 1581, St. Lucy's Day had come to
be celebrated on what is now December 23. Flemish
tradition remedies the matter by substituting St.
Thomas' Day (December 21) for St. Lucy's: *On St.
Thomas' the days lengthen* (Op St. Thomas lengen de
dagen). A widely known version of the Lucy proverb
expresses the thought in novel fashion, and seems to
have provided a model for other proverbs based on
days later in the winter:

On the festival of St. Lucy
The day grows by the leap of a flea.

('A la feste de Sainte Luce
Le jour croist du saut d'une puce'.)

The "leap of a flea" refers to the lengthening shadow
on the sun dial. At a later season (New Year's) the
measure is a cock's stride,[1] and when the proverb
ceased to be understood, it became *On Epiphany the
days lengthen by a cock's crow* (Op Driekoningendag
sijn de dagen een hanengekraai gelongen).

As a matter of fact, one argument advanced against
the introduction in 1581–82 of the Gregorian calendar
was that the weather proverbs based on saints' days
would no longer guide the husbandman. One of our
important early sources of calendar proverbs, *New
Lösstag. Nvtzliche bedencken vnd vnterscheidung der
pöflischen alten Lösstag, die feldregel vnd Bawrenpractic
angehend* (Rorschach am Bodensee, 1590), is designed
by its author to meet this very difficulty. The author,
Johann Rasch, kept some proverbs as they stood;
others he altered by the addition of the necessary ten
days. With a truly scientific spirit he printed both
the new and the old proverbs to show what he had
done.

In the proverbial weather forecast we discern four
essential elements which are associated in pairs: the
sign with its time of appearance, the weather with its

[1] See further examples in Beirens, "De folklore van het weer," *Neder-
landsch Tijdschrift voor Volkskunde*, XXIX (1924), 35–36.

time of appearance.[1] No importance attaches to the
order in which these pairs are coupled: we may have
Rain before seven stops before eleven, in which the
sign and its time of appearance come first, or *April
showers bring May flowers*, in which they follow. Of
course one or the other indication of time may be
implied rather than expressed, as in:

> Mackerel sky, mackerel sky,
> Never long wet, never long dry.

Only a few proverbs fix the time of the sign as New
Year's Day. Obviously they can have been invented
only after January 1 had become the first day of the
year.   Charlemagne, it will be remembered, had
moved the beginning of the year to March 1; the
Church dated the year from Easter. From the thirteenth century on, there were sporadic efforts to bring
the beginning of the year back to January 1, but the
movement was not generally successful until after the
Reformation, indeed not until the end of the sixteenth
century. Clearly the age of this small group of proverbs cannot be much greater than 350 years.

The forces which are operative in the creation of
weather proverbs are not altogether clear. Some seem
to reflect a principle of equalizing extremes of temperature: a warm summer balances a cold winter or
a green Christmas a white Easter. Although some
meteorologists claim quite positive periodicities, such

[1] Frick, "Le Peuple et la Prévision du Temps," *Schweizerisches Archiv
für Volkskunde*, XXVI (1926), 1 ff.

a principle seems to have little or no authority: over a long term of years the variations in temperature and rainfall are equalized, but the balance is not always restored within the space of twelve months. Etymological puns have a share in the invention of weather proverbs: the Russians say that flax should be sowed on St. Helena's Day (August 18). The maxim is obviously suggested by the similarity of Helena and "l'en" ('flax'). The association of St. Lucy and the winter solstice may possibly have some connection with the well-established association of Lucy and "lux" ('light'). In general, the love of rhyming does not appear to have created many weather proverbs, which, however, are like all other proverbs in the facility with which they use or imitate already existing proverbial types. A very curious adaptation of a saying which has originally no connection at all with the weather is seen in *Heute rot, morgen tot* ('Red to-day, dead to-morrow'), or *Morgen rot, abend tot* ('Red in the morning, dead at evening'), which in oral tradition signifies that a red morning is followed by a windless evening. This is a strange misapplication of a saying which ordinarily refers to the fate of soldiers.

Frick believes that traces of magic can be discerned in the oldest strata of weather proverbs, but as mankind has become more skeptical of magical powers the popularity of weather proverbs has declined. So far as we can see, few proverbs of the sort have been invented in the last three centuries. Perhaps one group, which can be termed local meteorological proverbs, deserves exemption: proverbs which refer to local signs may have developed more recently and often have a foundation in fact. A famous example of this sort is the passage at the beginning of *Wilhelm Tell* where the fisher, the hunter, and the shepherd are discussing the weather:

> Der graue Talvogt kommt, dumpf brüllt der Firn,
> Der Mythenstein zieht seine Haube an,
> Und kalt bläst es her aus dem Wetterloch;
> Der Sturm, ich mein', wird da sein, eh' wir's denken.

> ('The grizzly monarch of the vale is near,
> There's a deep muttering in the angry sky,
> Old Mytenstein puts on his cloudy cap,
> And icy blasts from the storm-cavern howl;
> Quicker than thought, the tempest will be here'.)
>
> ll. 38–41.[1]

English proverbs of the same sort exist, but of course enjoy only a very restricted circulation:

> When Billing Hill puts on its cap,
> Calverley Mill will get a slap;
> As long as Helsby (Hill) wears a hood,
> The weather's never very good.

The examination of Scotch weather proverbs of this sort shows that there is a considerable measure of truth and sound meteorology in them.[2]

---

1 The translation, published at Providence in 1838, is anonymous.
2 Dunwoody (*Weather Proverbs* [Signal Service Notes IX, Washington, 1883], pp. 9 ff.) reprints an article on this subject by Abercrombie and Marriott from the *Quarterly Journal of the Meteorological Society*.

Among others, the following examples are cited.
Clouds gathering on the tops of hills, although the
weather is otherwise clear, are a sign of rain:

> When Bredon Hill puts on his hat,
> Ye man of the vale, beware of that;
> When Cheviot ye see put on his cap,
> Of rain ye'll have a wee bit drap.

Windy cirrus clouds follow after a storm and betoken
wind rather than rain:

> Mackerel sky and mare's tails
> Make lofty ships to carry low sails.

Under certain special circumstances an unusually
clear atmosphere indicates rain: *The further the sight,
the nearer the rain.* All these, we are assured, rest upon
meteorological facts.

MEDICAL PROVERBS [1]

Another type of proverbial wisdom deals with
health and its maintenance. Like weather proverbs,

---

1 Such proverbs are not very abundant and have not been rendered easily
available for study. See bibliographies in Bonser, *Proverb Literature*
(London, 1930), pp. 432-433, Nos. 3778-3786, and pp. 439-442, Nos.
3839-3865a. The English proverbs are collected in a special section in
Bohn, *A Hand-book of Proverbs*, London, 1855 (almost this entire
section is taken from Ray's collection of 1670). Further materials are
brought together in Benham, *Book of Quotations, Proverbs and Household Words* (London, 1924), *s. v.* Health, and Lean, *Collectanea*, I,
478-509. Proverbs of various origins are translated into English in
W. K. Kelly, *Proverbs of All Nations* (1859), pp. 203-207; Christy,
Proverbs, Maxims, and Phrases of All Ages (1890), I, 489-492. There
are special books devoted to these proverbs, as follows. Catalan: Miró
y Borrás, *Aforística Médica Popular Catalana* (Manresa, 1900).

such maxims are not always easily distinguished from traditions and superstitions. Medical proverbs have in general aroused little interest, although everyone knows a rhyme like

> After dinner rest a while,
> After supper walk a mile.

This rhyme, which we can fairly call a proverb, traces its origin from a rule of the medical school of Salerno, the *Regimen Sanitatis Salernitanum*: Post coenam stabis vel passus mille meabis ('After dinner rest or walk a mile'), and has still older antecedents in the writings of Plutarch. We do not know the extent to which proverbial rules of health derive from this Latin handbook of medical lore. Inasmuch as it reached more than 150 editions and was widely translated, we might expect its influence to be consider-

Flemish: Thijm, *Kalender- en Gezondheidsregels* (Uitgaven der Koninklijke Vlaamsche Akademie, III, 9 [Ghent, 1893]). French: Couché, *Essai sur quelques Expressions Proverbiales et Sentences Populaires Relatives à la Médicine* (Paris, 1808). German: Bremser, *Medizinische Parömien* (Wien, 1806); Bücking, *Versuch einer Medicinischen und Physikalischen Erklärung Deutscher Sprichwörter und Sprichwörtlichen Redensarten* (Stendal, 1797); Ofellus, *Philosophie des Magens in Sprüchen aus Alter und Neuer Zeit* (Leipzig, 1886); Sepp, *Wichtige Gesundheitsregeln* (Augsburg, 1893). Italian: Bernoni, *L'Igiene della Tavola dalla Bocca del Popolo* (Venezia, 1872). Spanish: Monlau, *Elementos de Higiene Privada* (Madrid, 1870); Sorapan de Rieros, *Medicina Española Contenida en Proverbios Vulgares de Nuestra Lengua* (Granada, 1615–16). Curiously enough, several dissertations on medical proverbs were submitted to the University of Altdorf for the degree of Doctor of Medicine. I have noted nine in the first quarter of the eighteenth century; see Bonser, as above, Nos. 3844, 3847, 3848, 3853, 3854, 3858, 3861, 3862, 3865.

able. I have noted only a few survivals in oral tradition: *Plenus venter non studet libenter* ('A full stomach does not work willingly'), which we may compare with *Inanis venter non audit verba libenter* ('An empty stomach does not willingly listen'); *Contra vim mortis non est medicamen in hortis* (*Gegen den Tod ist kein Kraut gewachsen*, 'For death there is no medicine'). Clearly the *Regimen* is borrower in the case of *A tree is known by its fruit*, as in

> Fructibus ipsa suis, quae sit, dignoscitur arbor,
> Saepe solet similis filius esse patri.

Although this is not a health proverb, it may serve as an illustration of the other materials on which the *Regimen* draws.

A few health proverbs are international in their currency, but their number is apparently small. It is perhaps chance that I have noticed more examples of

> Milk before wine,
> I wish't were mine;
> Milk taken after
> Is poison's daughter

than of any other internationally known health proverb; the Germans say

> Wein auf Bier, das rat ich dir;
> Bier auf Wein, lass das sein;

the French,

> Lait sur vin est venin,
> Vin sur lait est souhait;

and the Spanish, *Dexo la lache al vino: bien seas venido,
amigo* ('Milk says to Wine, "Welcome, friend"').

What truth inheres in health proverbs remains to
be discovered; no one, so far as I am aware, has looked
into the matter. They have received thus far step-
motherly treatment at the hands of those interested
in proverbs, and the few books on health proverbs
which are named in the bibliographies are rarely significant contributions to the subject, unless the titles
and other indications wholly belie the contents. At
present we cannot make any generalizations regarding
the history, form, typical characteristics, or subject-
matter of these admonitions.

Health proverbs give the most varied kinds of advice. Some deal with sleep: *Six hours sleep for a man,
seven for a woman, and eight for a fool*; *Early to bed and
early to rise/Makes a man healthy, wealthy, and wise,*
which is at least as old as 1554: *Sanat, sanctificat et
ditat surgere mane*; *An hour's sleep before midnight is
worth two after.* A greater number, I suppose, deal
with food and eating: *You must eat a peck of dirt before
you die*; *An apple a day keeps the doctor away*; *Un œuf
n'est rien, deux font grand bien, trois est assez, quatre
est trop, cinq donnent la mort* ('One egg is nothing, two
are very good, three are enough, four are too much,
five will kill');[1] *Chair fait chair et poisson, poison*
('Meat makes flesh and fish, poison').[2] The play on

1 Le Roux de Lincy, II, 191; Polites, Παροιμίαι (Athens, 1899–1902),
III, 202.
2 Le Roux de Lincy, II, 205; Polites, II, 601–602.

the words "poisson" and "poison," which occurs again in *Poisson sans boisson est poison* ('Fish without drink is poison'), mark the forms as French. The proverb just quoted we find again in the English *Fish should swim thrice*, i. e. in water, sauce, and wine, and the belief involved is old: Petronius tells us in his famous description of a Roman banquet that "Fish should swim" (Pisces natare oportet).

So far as I can see, the more recently introduced articles of food do not give rise to proverbs: potatoes and coffee seem not to be mentioned. Tobacco has little or no place in proverbs. Butter, bread, meat, and cheese, on the other hand, appear frequently. *Bread and cheese* is traditionally a meal in English, and the French say *Fromage et pain est médecine au sain* ('Bread and cheese is medicine for the well'), and

> Pain et beurre et bon fromage
> contre la mort et le vray targe
>
> ('Bread and butter and good cheese
> are a true buckler against death'),

which is evidently closely related to the English *Bread and cheese be two targets against death*. So essential, indeed, is cheese that the French can say

> C'il qui mange du fromage,
> S'il ne le fait, il enrage
>
> ('He who does not eat cheese, will go mad'.)[1]

1 Le Roux de Lincy, II, 198.

Vegetables are rarely mentioned, although the French say

> Qui vin ne boit après salade
> est en danger d'être malade
>
> ('He who does not drink wine after
> his salad is in danger of falling sick')[1]

and the Scotch, *Good kail is half the meal*.

Some health proverbs give only general advice:

> Disne honnestement et soupe sobrement,
> Dors en hault et vivras longuement
>
> ('Dine rightly and sup moderately,
> Sleep upstairs and you will live long').[2]

I cannot say how well established is the superstition that sleeping upstairs is healthful. Familiar general advice in England is *An ague in the spring is physic for a king*; *Laugh and grow fat*. Occasionally we have an observation regarding the climate: *A green winter* (var. *Christmas*) *makes a fat churchyard*, which is evidently the model for *A hot May makes a fat churchyard*. Rare is such an observation as *Never rub your eye but with your elbow*, and prognostications are not usual:

> Quickly too'd ('toothed') and quickly go,
> Quickly will thy mother have moe.

---

1 Le Roux de Lincy, II, 216. Cf. Otto, *Archiv für Lateinische Lexicographie*, IV (1887), 351.
2 Le Roux de Lincy, II, 195; Wander, *Deutsches Sprichwörter-Lexikon*, V, col. 1545.

Some health proverbs are utterly obscure: *Parsley fried will bring a man to his saddle, and a woman to her grave*, which is evidently concerned with some superstition and may involve the aphrodisiac qualities of parsley. Only a very few proverbs concern themselves with the health of animals:

> Uphill spare me,
> Downhill forbear (*var.* ware) me,
> Plain way (*var.* level ground) spare me not,
> Nor let me drink when I am hot.

In general, proverbs concerned with physical peculiarities are rare.[1] Even those traditional sayings which describe or mock one's neighbors give little room to remarks on physical traits. It is worthy of note that proverbs mentioning physical traits are found most frequently among the Romance peoples. Recognition of such traits appears to be characteristic of a comparatively high culture which distinguishes individual details in the surrounding world; the savage and the peasant show little interest in physiognomic observations. Some traditional sentences

1 Hentig, "Physiognomik im Sprichwort," *Archiv für Kriminologie,* LXXX (1927), 136–144; Sartori, "Körperliche Merkmale im Westfälischen Volksmunde," *Volk und Rasse,* II (1927), 28–34; Bahlmann, "Der Menschliche Körper und seine Funktionen im Westfälischen Glauben, Brauch und Sprichwort," *Zeitschrift des Vereins für Rheinische und Westfälische Volkskunde,* XXIII (1926), 2–19, XXIV (1927), 46–52; Gittée, "De Volkshumor tegenover Lichamelijke Gebreken," *Volkskunde* (Ghent), VI (1893), 1–9; Otto, "Der menschliche Körper und seine Teile im [Lateinischen] Sprichwort," *Archiv für Lateinische Lexikographie,* VI (1889), 309–340; O. Scarlattini, *L'huomo e sue parte figurato e simbolico,* Augustae Vindelicorum, 1695.

relate physical attributes to psychical traits: *Curled heads are hasty*;

> Lange Nase, spitzes Kinn;
> Da sitzt der Teufel leibhaft drin
>
> ('Long nose, pointed chin;
> The Devil himself sits within');
>
> Cheshire born and Cheshire bred,
> Strong i' th' arm and weak i' th' head.

It might be possible to discover the extent to which sayings concerned with a relationship between physical and mental traits draw on the stock of physiological information associated with the Renaissance belief in "humours." The distrust and even fear of red hair is ancient and universal: *Rotbart nie gut ward* ('A red-beard was never good'), but the association with treason very probably involves an allusion to the traditional color of Judas's hair.[1] Apparently the proverbial warnings against red hair concern only a man. An analogous tradition, also of international currency, is *Crazy people don't turn gray, but asses are born gray* (De gekken grijsen niet, maar de ezels worden grijs geboren).[2] The lack of a beard or its scanty growth marks a man, particularly in southern lands, as suspicious. Certain physical traits are proverbially indices of other physical qualities, e. g. *Vir pilosus aut fortis aut luxuriosus* ('A hairy man, either

1 P. F. Baum, "Judas' Red Hair," *Journal of English and Germanic Philology*, XXI (1922), 520–529.
2 Hentig, *Archiv für Kriminologie*, LXXX (1927), 138.

strong or lustful'), and the traditional comparisons based on the length of nose or size of mouth. Typical illustrations of these proverbs, illustrations which are perhaps less offensive than most examples, have been collected to prove that the description of Juan Ruiz in an old Spanish poem contains more traditional elements and fewer bits of actual descriptive detail than we might at first believe.[1]

CONVENTIONAL PHRASES

Phrases and sentences customarily used in a single special situation form a special class of proverbs.[2] Although a metaphor is often present, its purpose is to describe the situation, not to convey an ethical or moral lesson. The Romans said *An ass from Aesop's pit* (Asinus de Aesopi puteo) of an unwelcome, noisy person. The allusion is entirely obscure. When the Scotch say *Either the tod* (fox) *or the bracken-bush* to silly people who speak vaguely and uncertainly, they are contracting an older proverb: *It is a blind goose that knoweth not a fox from a fern-bush.* The German sentence *An angel flew through the room* (Ein Engel

1 E. K. Kane, "The Personal Appearance of Juan Ruiz," *Modern Language Notes*, XLV (1930), 103–109.
2 I have noted special collections of conventional phrases only in Scandinavian languages; see, e. g., E. T. Kristensen, *Danske Ordsprog* (Copenhagen, 1890), pp. 532–555; anon., "Ordlekar från Åkers och Österrekarne Härader," *Bidrag til Södermanlands Äldre Kulturhistoria*, I, pt. 1 (1884), 94–99, II, pt. 6 (1886), 86–92; Nordlander, "Svenska Barnvisor ock Barnrim," *Nyare Bidrag till Kännedom om de Svenska Landsmålen*, V, pt. 5 (1886), pp. 254–280.

flog durchs Zimmer) is widely used of the sudden silence which falls on a social group, but its origin is not clear. Another equally obscure phrase with the same meaning is *Ein Leutnant bezahlt seine Schulden* ('A lieutenant pays his debts'), which has not yet found universal acceptance. In the same situation the Dutch say "The pastor is going by" (De domine gaat voorbi) and Americans say "Quaker meeting" or "It's twenty minutes past." *Let her go, Gallagher* is, I believe, unexplained.

Many fixed, conventional phrases exist in English: *I have other fish to fry*, i. e. 'I cannot undertake a proposed task'; *His eyes are bigger than his stomach*, i. e. 'he cannot eat all he asked for'; *Boys will be boys*, i. e. 'a boyish prank is a minor fault and one to be overlooked'; *You're the doctor*, i. e. 'you, the more competent person, and not I, should make the decision'; *Sent a boy to mill*, said when a low card, which the player thought high enough to win the trick, is exceeded by the opponent; *Heads I win, tails you lose*, said of an undertaking in which only one participant profits; *It's six of one and half a dozen of the other* or *It's as broad as it's long*, said when there is no reason for preferring either of two alternatives; *What's yours is mine and what's mine is my own*, said of a selfish child; *Fingers were made before forks*; *Take while the taking is good*, said to a person who hesitates to accept something when it is offered; *Put that in your pipe and smoke it*, said as impudent repartee; *That's no skin off my elbow*, i. e. *My withers are unwrung*, 'the event or remark does not injure or refer to me'; *Keep that under your hat*; *Do as I say and not as I do*, which has parallels in Livy and the New Testament. *Tell it to the marines!* which may be compared to the Horatian *Credat Judaeus Apella* ('Let the Jew Apella believe it,' *Sat.* 1, 5, 100), a "learned" proverb, was parodied for a season as "Tell it to the Danes," when F. A. Cook's story of the discovery of the North Pole was accepted by the Danish Academy.

Generally speaking, such fixed phrases as we are now considering rarely deal with superstitions. The ordinary English form of refusal to give the name of one's informant is *A little bird told me*, while on the continent it is *My little finger* (var. *thumb*) *told me* (*Mein kleiner Finger* [var. *Daumen*] *hat es mir gesagt*). The third witch in *Macbeth* alludes to the superstition underlying the continental phrase, but her remark is hardly proverbial in form:

> By the pricking of my thumbs,
> Something wicked this way comes.
>
> Act iv, sc. 1.

Ask me no questions and I'll tell you no lies is a brutally frank formula with the same general meaning. Old and widespread is the phrase *A hair of the dog that bit you* for a drink of liquor taken on the morning after a night of dissipation. It displays curious and typical variations: Ben Jonson says in *Bartholomew Fair* "pluck a hair of the same wolf" and Hermann Kurz, a German poet of the nineteenth century, alludes to the hair of a cat in a similar connection. These variations illustrate once more the substitution of analogous and contrary details in oral tradition. In both these examples of superstitions in fixed phrases we have very ancient and widely known tradition.

Evasive descriptions of childbirth have in some cases become standing formulae.[1] The stork is proverbial in English, and the German phrase is even more specific: *The stork has bitten mother's leg* (Der Storch hat der Mutter ins Bein gebissen). A wholly satisfactory explanation is not forthcoming. Obviously the phrase cannot have been invented in England, where storks are rarely, if ever, seen. There may be some primitive symbolism in the mention of the stork. Another form, which is characteristically English, but has not spread to America, assigns the origin of children to the parsley bed; it is equally inexplicable. A more careful examination of the superstitions and medical lore associated with parsley would probably throw light on the matter. An analogous German tradition names the cabbage bed, and is very likely connected more or less directly with the English phrase.

[1] See the collectanea entitled "Woher kommen die Kinder," *Am Urquell*, IV (1893), 224 ff.; V (1894), 80 f., 162, 254, 255, 287; VI (1895), 41, 125, 159, 218 f.; H. F. Feilberg, *Bidrag til en Ordbog over Jyske Almuesmål, s. v.* Barn (see also Tillæg); Boekenoogen, "Waar de Kinderen vandaar Komen," *Volkskunde* (Ghent), XXII (1911), 18–24, 143–151, 193–198, XXIII (1912), 29–37.

Proverbial Prophecies

A few proverbs forecast the future in politics or war. Perhaps the most famous example is *Austria erit ultima in orbe* ('Austria shall be the last thing in the world') or, arranged in the order of the vowels, *Austria erit in orbe ultima*. English proverbs are particularly concerned with military affairs: *He that England will win must with Scotland* (var. *Ireland*) *begin*; *The vale of Holmsdale was never won and never shall*;

> When the black fleet of Norway is come and gone,
> England, build houses of lime and stone,
> For afterwards you shall have none;

> When hemp is spun,
> England is done.

> Nene and Welland
> Shall drown all Holland.

Spenser knew the last of these prophecies. Such sayings are probably fragments of mediaeval or later prophecies; we might understand them better if the whole were before us. Some chance has dictated the preservation of these prophecies. A still more curious prophecy was current in Germany before the recent war and during its early years:

> 1911 ein Flutjahr,
> 1912 ein Blutjahr.

When the Balkan War scare of 1912 passed over, the rhyme could of course no longer serve as a prophecy and it was revised to read:

> 1911 ein Flutjahr,
> 1912 ein gut Jahr,
> 1913 ein Blutjahr.

And still further additions and alterations were needed in the further course of events. So far as we may see in proverbs a summing up of a prevailing popular mood, this proverb illustrates the fatalistic attitude which preceded the war of 1914.

III

THE STYLE OF PROVERBS

ALTHOUGH rigidity of form constitutes an essential characteristic of proverbs, scholarly efforts to describe and study it have been unavailing and profitless. Metrical studies have been uniformly tedious and uninspired. The examination of other important stylistic factors has not yielded important results. We may consider the proverbial vocabulary: a few words are interesting as relics of former days, and a few others as nonce-formations. In the main, however, proverbs are rarely distinguished by peculiarities in diction. They must necessarily restrict their choice of words to the simplest and most obvious materials. Except for Heusler's remarks concerning the stylistic differences between the Viking proverb and the humbler vulgar proverb and the previous mention of *Faint heart ne'er won fair lady* as an instance of stylistic contrast, the question of proverbial style as a reflection of the speaker's social background has been neglected. Still other matters call for our attention. Although the rhetorical details in proverbs have been often discussed, the subject is not exhausted. The figures of speech, notably contrast and metaphor, and the kinds of sentences used in proverbs are especially interesting bits of rhetoric. Certain proverbial types which are important for their origin, history, or peculiarities may be distinguished on stylistic grounds. And finally, I shall discuss the subject of proverbs in their literary relations, a subject which extends beyond the merely stylistic in its importance.

Metrical studies of proverbs have rarely escaped the temptation to employ the elaborate classical system of metrics, and have consequently failed to discover the essential traits.[1] The chances of winning significant results in this field are good, if hairsplitting classical metrical formulae are avoided. As we might expect, proverbs conform to the general rhythm of the language in which they have been taken down. So far as we can determine and describe the prevailing rhythm of a language we have a standard with which we can compare each individual proverb. It might be possible, in the case of a proverb borrowed from another language, to trace a gradual adaptation to a new rhythm of speech. Conceivably we might find in similar fashion a development in the passage from the mediaeval to the modern vernacular proverb, a development which avoided certain metrical types and preferred others. The importance of such conclusions for the history of metrics and poetics — if they can be established — is obvious. Of course we must deal

1 See Seiler, *Deutsche Sprichwörterkunde* (Munich, 1922), pp. 194 ff.

with deep currents in linguistic and stylistic habits, and the investigation must be conducted in such a way as to emphasize broad tendencies.

The metrical device of alliteration is an untrustworthy mark of age in a proverb. Alliteration is a familiar characteristic of early Germanic verse, and for a long time scholars regarded alliterative formulae as ancient.[1] A long list of such formulae will be found in the early pages of Grimm's *Deutsche Rechtsalter-tümer*. We are no longer tempted to regard an alliterative formula or proverb as necessarily reaching back to that early period in Germanic literary history when alliterative verse prevailed. Some alliterative phrases are old, while others have arisen in much more recent times from the love of a jingle. There is no easy way to distinguish between old and new alliterative expressions; we are forced to rely largely on the historical evidence. Alliteration is not sufficient to prove the antiquity of a proverb: *Many men, many minds* is a classical and not an early Germanic proverb. An investigation of the facts concerning alliteration in proverbs would begin by discussing what signs prove a phrase to be old. With stylistic, chronological, linguistic, and other tests at our disposal, we might learn that there are two groups of alliterative proverbs, one old and one new, with different characteristics. In such an investigation one must bear constantly in mind that apt alliteration's artful aid marks

1 See pp. 89 ff.

both simple speech, as we see in children's rhymes, and highly elaborated diction.

The typical form of the mediaeval Latin proverb is the leonine hexameter: *Arbor per primum quaevis non corruit ictum* ('A tree does not fall at the first stroke'); *Parvus pendetur fur, magnus abire videtur* ('The little thief is hanged, the big one is seen to go off'). These examples, which have been chosen merely because we have already referred to them above, illustrate a conspicuous fault of such proverbs. In order to fill the hexameter, the versifier adds useless words: "quaevis, videtur." Even clumsier expansion is seen in *Ius est implere promissa decentia vere* ('Promise is debt') or *Auri natura non sunt splendentia plura* ('All is not gold that glitters'), and occasionally a whole clause is needed to fill the line: *Sunt pueri pueri, vivunt pueriliter illi* ('Boys will be boys'); *Luscus praefertur caeco, sic undique fertur* ('Better the eye to be sore than all blind'); *Res miranda nova, picae fur abstulit ova* ('An egg is stolen even from a witch'); *Quod male lucratur, male perditur et nihilatur* ('Ill gotten, ill spent'). Even when the composer had a brief and effective model in classical Latin before him, he did not hesitate: *Quot homines, tot sententiae* ('Many men, many minds') yields *Quolibet in capite viget ingenium speciale*. Although a stylistic examination of proverbs in leonine hexameters leads into arid and untrodden fields, it is worth undertaking. No one has sought to learn what standards existed, whether proverbs were actually

composed in this form in addition to being translated
from the vernacular, or what local stylistic variations
and habits or developments in the form can be found.
It has been pointed out, for example, that leonine
hexameters with feminine rhymes are probably later
in origin than those with masculine rhymes.[1] Altogether useless are the emendations which Suringar[2]
and Seiler[3] make to correct the versification of these
mediaeval Latin proverbs. The versifiers gave little
thought to such matters: some wrote carefully and
others not.

The linguistic peculiarities of proverbs have never
received thorough examination.[4] As we have seen,
old or dialectal words are kept. New words which go
beyond the ordinary bounds of word-formation are
occasionally found. *He is one of the McTak's, not one
of the McGie's* rests on the pun involved in "McGie"
and the family name McGee. The compound McTak
is unusual, indeed unnatural, for the component Mc-
is never used with a verb. German seems to make
new compounds more freely than English, and the
results in proverbs are more interesting. *Ein Kauf-
mann ist kein Schenkmann* illustrates the readiness
with which "Mann" is used as second member in

1 See Kock and Petersen, *Ostnordiska och Latinska Medeltidsordspråk*
 (Copenhagen, 1889–94), II, 65.
2 *Over de* "Proverbia Communia" (Leiden, 1863).
3 *Deutsche Sprichwörterkunde, passim.*
4 See Seiler, as above, p. 179. Tetzner (*Die Wortbildung im Deutschen
 Sprichwort*, Gelsenkirchen, 1908) includes many plays on words which
 can scarcely have been proverbial.

compounds; normally "Mann" is compounded with
another noun, e. g. "Amtmann," "Fuhrmann," but
in this case the speaker has regarded "Kauf-" as derived from the verb "kaufen" and not from the noun
"Kauf," and has formed an analogous, but new and
unusual, compound "Schenkmann" from the verb
"schenken." The punning proverb *Vorrat ist besser
als Nachrat* is comparable to the English *Hindsight
is better than foresight*. In both instances the noun
which served as a basis, i. e. "Vorrat," 'foresight,'
has yielded a new compound with a first member of
opposite meaning. "After wit" in *After wit is dear
bought* is a nonce-form of similar origin; it is of course
a compound word and should be so printed, although
the collections print it otherwise. New words are
made in ways which are no longer used: *Many a
mickle makes a muckle* contains the word "muckle"
formed by vowel gradation from "mickle" in the
same way that "sing" and "sung" are related. New
formations are especially frequent in coining whimsical place-names for proverbial use. With one place-
name as a model a second one is invented for the
sake of contrast: *Er stammt nicht aus Schenkendorf,
sondern aus Greifswald* ('He does not come from
Giversville but from Graspers' Grove'). So, too, the
historical proverb *Nimmweg, Reissweg und Unrecht*
('Take away, snatch away, and injustice') twists the
names Nimwegen (the final *n* is silent), Ryswick, and
Utrecht to describe the treaties of 1678, 1697, and

1713. Such nonce-proverbs are widely used in Germany, but are not so familiar elsewhere. The English proverbs *He is none of the Hastings*, i. e. 'he is slow,' and *He was born at Little Wittham* illustrate a similar punning use of a proper name, but contain no new formations. With them we may compare the German "Drückeberger" ('one who avoids an issue or responsibility') and "Schlauberger" ('a person who is adroit in attaining his ends'); "Schlaumeier," which has the same meaning as "Schlauberger," is a different kind of formation, since it does not suggest a place-name.

The figures in proverbs have not been studied profitably. An application of the classical rhetorical rules and subdivisions will hardly bring to light anything of interest or importance.[1] Seiler tries another tack. He distinguishes three classes of metaphors in proverbs: (1) proverbs in which the idea preceded the image, e. g. *Those who will live in glass houses should not throw stones*; (2) those in which the image preceded the idea, e. g. *New brooms sweep clean*; (3) those in which the image and the idea are conceived simultaneously, e. g. *Still waters run deep*. The first group is recognizable, he asserts, by its employment of an impossible image: glass houses do not exist. A collection and a close study of proverbs in which an impossible situation is described would certainly be fruitful.

1 See the literature, which is rather discouraging in its achievements, in Seiler, *Deutsche Sprichwörterkunde*, pp. 153 ff.

Seiler is perhaps inclined to go a little too far in regarding a situation as impossible: *Too many cooks
spoil the broth* can hardly be considered as depicting
an impossible situation. The distinction between the
second and third groups is, as Seiler acknowledges,
entirely metaphysical and is therefore better discarded. Proverbs develop from the generalization of a
simple scene, and it is useless to discuss whether the
perception of the scene and its application are simul-
taneous or separated in time.

Simple metaphors which verge on personification
are of course common to proverbs in all lands: ab-
stractions are assigned the powers of human beings,
e. g. *Truth will out*; *Lies have short legs*; *Walls have ears*
(compare *Campus habet oculos, silva aures*); *Hunger
breaks stone walls*; *Misery loves company*; *Hunger is
the best cook*. A freer use of personification and in
a form which is more dramatically effective marks
German proverbs, e. g. *Trauwohl reitet das Pferd weg*
('Easymark rides off with the plug,' i. e. 'the trusting
man is cheated'); *Herr Pfennig geht voran* ('Mr.
Penny heads the procession'); *Borghard ist Lehn-
hards Knecht* ('Mr. Borrow is the servant of Mr.
Lend'), which involves a pun on the family names
"Borghard" and "Lehnhard." The type is infrequent in English, e. g. *Brag is a good dog, but Holdfast
a better*. Apparently the popularity of such proverbs
in which a whole scene is dramatized without naming
an abstraction — although the abstraction is the

subject of the proverb — has declined in modern use. The proverbs in which it appears in most characteristic form are not frequently used; no new proverbs, so far as I can see, are being made on the same model. As is evident, the history of this stylistic device is unknown. In fact, we know very little about the development and spread of any particular stylistic peculiarities in proverbs.

A rhetorical trait which is found in the simplest proverbs, even in those simple aphorisms which do not rise to the dignity of a metaphor, is parallelism of structure with its almost inevitable accompaniment, contrast. Parallelism and contrast are found in words, structure, and thought. Simple proverbial forms like *Many men, many minds*; *Like master, like man*; *The more he has, the more he wants*; *Nothing venture, nothing win*; *Testis unus, testis nullus* are dominated by parallelism. The repetition of the same word in two phrases heightens the effect of the contrasting second members. Many proverbs employ contrast alone by separating contrasting words with a colorless predicate: *Hindsight is better than foresight*; *The longest way round is the shortest way home.* A more complicated use of these devices is seen in *Young saint, old devil*; *Man proposes, God disposes*; *The nearer the church, the farther from God*; *Spare the rod and spoil the child*; *Where ignorance is bliss, 'tis folly to be wise.* Here we have parallelism of structure used to emphasize the contrast in words. *Where ignorance is bliss*, *'tis folly to be wise* illustrates a chiastic use of contrast with parallelism of structure.

The stylistic peculiarities of very brief proverbs offer problems which have not yet been seriously attacked. Archbishop Trench conjectures [1] that those sayings which lack a verb are characteristic of classical tradition: Χρήματ' ἀνήρ ('Money [makes] the man'); [2] *Sus Minervam* ('The sow [teaches] Minerva,' i. e. 'the fool claims the ability to teach the learned'); *Fures clamorem* ('Thieves [fear] uproar'). He is of course well aware of *Forewarned, forearmed*, which is *Praemonitus, praemunitus*, and he praises the terseness of *Voll, toll* ('A drunken man is a mad man'). It is by no means certain that we may venture to assign proverbs of this form to any one source. No doubt they originated in different ways: *Sus Minervam* may very well be the residuum of a lost fable, and Χρήματ' ἀνήρ represents an old aphoristic sentence type which we cannot use now. Heusler[3] observes that the disinclination to use this old aphoristic form like the German *Viel Feind, viel Ehr* ('Many enemies, much honor') or the English *Young saint, old devil* makes itself felt in the early Middle Ages in Icelandic literature. The form has not been able to maintain itself with any notable success. Yet there are proverbs

1 *On the Lessons in Proverbs*, p. 17.
2 Attributed to Alcæus. Cf. Erasmus, *Chiliades*, ed. 1598, p. 563; Burckhardt, *Arabic Proverbs* (London, 1830), p. 198, No. 680.
3 *Altgermanische Dichtung* (Handbuch der Literaturwissenschaft), p. 68, § 61.

made on this model which, I conjecture, are not very ancient, e. g. *Good hand, good hire*, a phrase which is used of a farm laborer employed only at rush seasons. The proverbs which contain no verb but are held together by correlatives, e. g. *The more, the merrier; The fewer, the better fare*, may be mentioned. The brevity of Russian proverbs, on which Altenkirch [1] comments, is of a different sort, and illustrates what can be accomplished in compression by a language which has no article, which dispenses with the verb "to be" in the present tense, and which employs a very condensed participial idiom.

The rhetorical device of connecting two abstract ideas in terms of a family relationship appears to spring originally from Greek personifications of abstract qualities. Directly or indirectly, the many classical Latin examples seem to imitate Greek constructions. Homer (*Iliad*, xvi, 231) calls sleep the brother of death, and Virgil (*Aen.*, vi, 278) repeats the thought. Apuleius wrote "Poverty . . . is the discoverer of all the arts" (Paupertas . . . omnium artium repertrix, *De Magia* [*Apologia*], 18), a phrase which may have been only an epigram to its author but one which has given rise to the most familiar of all proverbs made on this model: *Necessity is the mother of invention*. From the very beginning this rhetorical device keeps a level a few degrees above the unmistakable popular proverb so that we are

[1] *Archiv für Slavische Philologie*, XXX (1909), 19.

always a little conscious of art in its use. The Ter-
entian "Subservience begets friends, truth hatred"
(Obsequium amicos, veritas odium parit) was often
quoted, if it was not actually proverbial, and its similarity to *Familiarity breeds contempt* is obvious. The
two sayings are combined, of course in their Latin
forms, by Pope Innocent III; and not content with
that, Angelo Poliziano reports a still longer version
which springs from the same root: "Veritas odium,
prosperitas superbiam, securitas periculum, famili-
aritas contemptum, id est, parit" ('Truth breeds
hate, prosperity pride, safety danger, familiarity contempt'). The notion that fame brings envy in its
train finds expression in "Invidia gloriae comes [est],"
and Seneca and St. Jerome said "Vicina sunt vitia
virtutibus" ('Vices are neighbors of virtues'), which
is of similar form. Quintillian has "Avarice is the
mother of cruelty" (Crudelitatis mater avaritia est).
The variety and freedom with which the formula is
used in these early instances are worthy of note, and
seem to indicate that it was by no means a rigid
rhetorical convention.

In later periods, particularly after the Renaissance,
the number of examples of the form increases greatly
in the handbooks of apothegms and sententious remarks, but the formula, which rarely occurs in proverbs collected in oral tradition, has little elasticity and
is, with one or two exceptions, an outworn frame-
work with no popular associations. The Rule of St.

Benedict has *Discretio mater virtutis* ('Discretion is the mother of virtue'), which is evidently the model for the popular Italian proverb *Discretion is the mother of asses* (La discrezione è la madre degli asini).[1] Heinrich Bebel, a German humanist and the first man to record (although in Latin) German proverbs, has *Veritas temporis filia* ('Truth is the daughter of time'), and Angelo Poliziano, an Italian humanist of the preceding generation, *La notte è madre de pensieri* ('Night is the mother of thoughts'), a thought which is more simply expressed as *In nocte consilium*. Notwithstanding the evidence of the Italian parody of the Rule of St. Benedict, almost all proverbs on this model have an artificial, bookish sound, and rarely occur in collections derived from oral sources. The legal proverb *Actio est filia obligationis* ('The act is the daughter of the obligation') seems a learned maxim rather than a traditional proverb. I give by way of conclusion some phrases which are cited with more or less plausibility as traditional proverbs: *Pity is akin to love*; *Ingratitude is the daughter of pride*; *Diligence is the mother of good luck*; *Idleness is hunger's mother and theft's brother* (Ledigheid is hongers moeder en van dieverij een broeder), which seems to belong to a widely distributed group represented by the English and French proverb *Idleness is the mother of all the vices* (L'ennui est mère de toutes les vices); *Experience is the mother of wisdom*; *Ignorance is the mother of devotion* (var.

1 Wesselski, *Poliziano*, p. 244, No. 398.

impudence); *Sorrow is laughter's daughter*; *Disuse is sister to abuse*. I have made no effort to collect examples outside of English and the classical languages, although the type is a familiar one in all the languages of western Europe, e. g. *Distrust is the mother of safety* (La défiance est mère de sureté),[1] the Low German *Luck is luck's mother* (Glück is glückes moder),[2] or the whimsical *Vorsicht ist die Mutter der Porzellankiste* ('Caution is the mother of the porcelain chest'). The actual contribution made by the formula to the traditional proverbial stock is slight: *Necessity is the mother of invention*, which is actually one of the earliest recorded instances of the type, stands almost alone except for *The thought is father to the deed*.

Another proverbial type is distinguished by the use of correlatives, e. g. *Ubi timor, ibi pudor* ('Where there is fear, there is modesty') — which is first reported in Greek; *Ubi amici, esse ibidem opes* ('Where friends are, there also is wealth'). Although the examples in the Greek and Latin classics are not numerous, they seem to have provided the models for a rather abundant development in the Middle Ages, a

1 Quitard, *Dictionnaire des Proverbes* (Paris, 1842), p. 290.
2 See the many German examples collected in Seiler, *Deutsche Sprichwörterkunde*, p. 155. See also the Dutch *God wolts is alder bede moeder* ('"Would to God" is the mother of all prayers,' *Proverbia communia*, No. 354) and *Voorzigtigheid is de moeder der wijsheid* ('Caution is the mother of wisdom'). The first of these is the only example in the 803 proverbs in the late fifteenth-century *Proverbia communia*. Perhaps the form had not yet established itself.

development which, to be sure, accorded with the native genius of Latin and Greek. Characteristic mediaeval examples of the type are: *Ubi crux, ibi lux* ('Where the Cross is, there is light'); *Ubi mala fortuna, ibi mala fides* ('Where there is bad luck, there is bad faith'); and the expanded form: *Ubi timor, ibi pudor; ubi pudor, ibi honor* ('Where there is fear, there is modesty; where there is modesty, there is honor'). We may perhaps see the difference between this type and the modern traditional proverb in the contrast between *Ubi bona custodia, ibi bona pax* ('Where there is good guarding, there peace is kept') and *Good fences make good neighbors*. Modern representatives of the type are not very frequent, but we may note such familiar proverbs as *Where there's a will, there's a way*; *Where there's smoke, there's fire*. The relative popularity of the type appears from the list in Bohn's *Handbook of [English] Proverbs*, where the proverbs are arranged alphabetically according to the first words: those beginning with "where" are not especially abundant.

Other correlatives are used somewhat less often. We have classical models in *Qualis dominus, talis et servus* ('Like master, like man') from Petronius, which is the model for *Qualis hera, tales pedissaeque* ('Like mistress, like maid'), and the Plautine *Quot homines, tot sententiae* ('As many men, so many opinions'), and furthermore in *Qualis grex, talis rex* ('Like company, like king') and *Qualis homo, talis sermo* ('Like man, like speech'). A humanistic imitation is *Quot regiones, tot mores* ('As many regions, so many customs'). The modern languages have few correlatives or, at least, few correlatives which translate neatly and effectively the Latin formulae. Even when it was possible to translate *ubi* . . ., *ibi* . . . satisfactorily, modern tradition has generally failed to take advantage of the opportunity. For *quot* . . ., *tot* . . . there is no translation which rings true in popular speech; and consequently *Quot homines, tot sententiae* becomes *Many men, many minds.* The effect of the correlatives is produced by parallelism. It might perhaps be maintained that correlatives live on in such proverbs as *The nearer the church, the farther from God;* but the parallel structure and the contrast of "nearer" and "farther" rather than the correlatives "the . . ., the . . ." hold the proverb together.

Forms which are characteristic of Germanic proverbs have not as yet been generally recognized. An old type began with the words "One must" (or "ought") and was perhaps a general Germanic type.[1] In fact, we can see in Icelandic a still older formula which had no subject: *At kveldi skal dag leyfa* ('At evening one should praise the day,' *Hávamál*, 81, 1). When, however, the use of "skal" without a subject became less natural and idiomatic, the indefinite pronoun was used as subject. In the Germanic languages

---

1 Taylor, "The proverbial formula *Man soll* . . .," *Zeitschrift für Volks-kunde*, XL (1930), 152–156.

in which the indefinite pronoun is little used in popular speech, as in English, the formula necessarily fell
into disuse. The formula "mon sceal" is frequent in
Old English didactic verse, and the freedom of its use
suggests its proverbial popularity then. The disappearance of the formula is almost complete in Middle
English. The Middle English *Proverbs of Hendyng*
have *Under boske shal men weder abide*, and those who
used it may have understood "men" as plural. In the
German Middle Ages the formula seems not to have
enjoyed particular favor, although instances are not
entirely wanting: the proverb *Turn your coat according to the wind* finds formulation in the later Middle
Ages as *Man sol den mantel keren nach der wind wehet.*
Modern German still uses sayings of this type, e. g.
Man soll den Tag nicht vor dem Abend loben. Since the
formula so readily lends itself to various uses, it is
often difficult to know whether we are dealing with a
sententious remark, a maxim, or a proverb.

Along with the disappearance of proverbial types,
we must also reckon with the possibility of the creation of new patterns. It will require some study to
prove that a new pattern has been created, and no one
has yet made such an attempt. It is entirely conceiv-
able, for example, that the declarative sentence beginning with "You" is a new pattern, e. g. *You can't
spoil a rotten egg*; *You can never tell till you've tried*;
*You can lead a horse to water but you can't make him
drink.* I am inclined to believe that early examples of

this pattern are not frequent and that the form now enjoys a greater popularity and wider use than ever before. Obviously the formula with "You" replaces older impersonal forms like *There's small choice in rotten apples*; *It's ill halting before a cripple*; *One may live and learn*.

Details of style often give a hint regarding the age or the history of a proverb, but our methods of study and the criteria on which we can rely are as yet little developed. Rhyme, alliteration, idiom, or peculiar verbal tricks of style often mark a version in one language as the source of a version in another. Of these indications, rhyme and alliteration are less reliable than idiom.

Ordinarily the rhymed proverb is the source of the unrhymed proverb: *Mieux vaut en paix un œuf, qu'en guerre un bœuf* yields *Besser ein Ei im Frieden als ein Ochs im Kriege* ('An egg in peace is better than an ox in wartime'); and *Les morts ont toujours tort* gives *Die Toten haben immer Unrecht* ('The dead are always wrong'). The rule is not without exceptions: *Morgenstunde hat Gold im Munde* is not the original form because it is rhymed or because it alliterates. *Necessity knows no law* and *Not kennt kein Gebot* are both translations of *Necessitas dat legem*. *A friend in need is a friend indeed* illustrates how a proverb is padded to obtain a rhyme. The employment of useless words for metrical purposes is especially frequent in mediaeval Latin proverbs in leonine hexameters. Appropriately enough, one collection, which belongs to the end of the eleventh or the beginning of the twelfth century, entitles itself: *Proverbia Rusticorum Mirabiliter Versificata*, although the humor which we see in the name was entirely unconscious.

The effort to produce a rhyming formula, as, for example, in the transformation of *Fortis ut mors dilectio* ('Love [is] as strong as death') into *Amour et mort, rien n'est plus fort*, is often very successful. Abraham à Sancta Clara, court preacher in Vienna in the last quarter of the seventeenth century, displayed a great fondness for rhyming epigrams and proverbs. He was, it will be remembered, the model for Schiller's Capuchin in *Wallensteins Lager*. Abraham's native liking for rhymes and puns makes it hard to know whether his sayings are actually proverbial: "Ehestand, Wehestand" ('The state of marriage [is] a state of misery') is no doubt his own invention. In the case of "Man thut halt die grossen Dieb perdoniren, und die kleinen stranguliren" ('The big thieves are pardoned and the little ones strangled'), which is his version of *Die kleinen Diebe hängt man und die grossen lässt man laufen* ('The little thieves are hanged and the big ones are allowed to run away'), we cannot readily discover how wide an acceptance the rhymed form enjoyed. Whatever the status of this illustration may really be, oral tradition is very likely to make such changes in order to find a rhyme. *Homo proponit, Deus disponit* ('Man proposes, God disposes') yields a rhyming proverb readily enough in English and the Romance languages; the Germans say *Der Mensch denkt und Gott lenkt*; the Dutch, *De mensch wikt, maar God beschikt*; and the Swedish *Menniskan spår och Gud rår*. Clearly the Latin rhyme was a model in the invention of these proverbs. *Sauf oder lauf* ('Drink or run') is evidently translated from the Ciceronian "Aut bibat aut abeat," and it in turn is Ἢ πῖθι ἢ ἄπιθι.

A play on words or an allusion often identifies the age or home of a proverb. Clearly *While there's life, there's hope* comes from the Latin *Dum spiro, spero* ('While I breathe, I hope'), although the force of the English proverb is somewhat different from that of the Latin. *Forewarned, forearmed* is the Latin *Praemonitus, praemunitus*. *Amore, more, ore, re firmantur amicitiae* ('Friendships are strengthened by love, manners, the mouth, and deed'), which is perhaps an ingenious rhetorical invention rather than a proverb, can only be Latin, and the use of rhyme shows, furthermore, that it is a mediaeval construction. The allusion to gender in *Le parole son femine, e fatti son maschi* ('Words are feminine; deeds are masculine') [1] has a point in Italian which it would not have in German or English. In *Acht is meer dan duizend* ('Eight [also: 'care, watchfulness'] is more than a dozen') [2] the pun is possible only in Dutch or German

1 Wesselski, *Poliziano*, p. 214.
2 Stoett, *Nederlandsche Spreekwoorden* (Zutphen, 1923–25), No. 45.

and identifies the home of the proverb. There is no mistaking the source of the Swedish *Föra swin til Rhin, det blijr antå swin* ('Lead a pig to the Rhine; it remains a pig'),[1] in which the need of a rhyme preserves the proper name. Such allusions to places or persons often give us invaluable hints: *Die Zeit ist vorbei, da Bertha spann* ('The time is past, when Bertha span') must be a translation of *Ce n'est plus le temps que Berthe filoit*. An unusual, obsolete, or foreign idiom is ordinarily an insuperable handicap to a proverb and causes its early disappearance. There are nevertheless instances in which the idiom tells the origin of a proverb. The Bohemian *Když ovce pošly, i kozy ke cti přišli* ('Where sheep are lacking, the goats are honored')[2] preserves, we are told, a German idiom in the second clause. The Middle High German *Zwêne sint eines her* ('Two are an army for one,' i. e. 'two can overpower one') soon became unintelligible in German and the proverb disappeared from use. It has been conjectured that *her* 'army' was construed as *Herr* 'master' and that the phrase *Herr werden eines Dinges*, 'to become master of a thing,' arose from the proverb. Although the principle involved in this explanation is correct, the absence of a direct connection between the two phrases and the readiness with which the second could have developed independently (as in English) make the explanation improbable.

1 Krohn, *Die Folkloristische Arbeitsmethode* (Oslo, 1926), p. 139.
2 Altenkirch, *Archiv für Slavische Philologie*, XXX (1909), 13, 321–322.

Proverbs are of course distinguished by individual stylistic traits. It is perhaps more difficult for us to discern the characteristic traits in proverbs which are familiar to us. Foreign and unusual forms are easily recognized. Two such forms will be described as illustrations of the possible variations in proverbial style. One of these forms, the dialogue proverb, is Levantine in its distribution and has found only chance acceptance in Western Europe. The other form, a special type of epigrammatic proverb, enjoyed a remarkable popularity in Europe after the Renaissance, but it is no longer in particular favor.

Dialogue Proverbs

A very curious proverbial form which is utterly strange to us is that of a brief dialogue. A typical instance, which has been taken down in Greek, Ruthenian, and Russian, is *How sweet the milk is! — Where did you see it? — My uncle saw another man drinking it on the other side of the river.* Even more widely distributed is the dialogue: *I have caught a bear. — Bring it here. — It won't come. — Then come yourself. — It won't let me go.* The Poles have altered the proverb by substituting a Tartar for the bear. A similar form is the Arabic *They said to the camel-bird* (the ostrich), *"Carry." It answered, "I cannot, for I am a bird." They said, "Fly." It answered, "I cannot, for I am a camel."* Others are *They brought the wolf to school and read "A, B, C" to him; but he said,*

"*Lamb, she-goat, kid*"; and *They said to the lazy man,* "*Today is a holiday.*" *Then he answered,* "*Tomorrow and the day after, too.*" The European equivalent is *Lazy people always have holidays* (Ignavis semper feriae). The fact that family quarrels are often marked by bitterness is thus expressed: *Who knocked out your eye? — My brother. — That's why the blow went so deep.* The saying *The Lord helps those who help themselves* is *St. John, help me! — Put out your hand yourself.* This unfamiliar form can be converted into the ordinary European type. The French *The ass invited to a wedding ought to bring wood or water* (Asne convié à nopces eau ou boys y doibt aporter) [1] probably retains a trace of the original Arabic narrative form: *They asked the ass,* "*Whither?*" *He answered,* "*To fetch wood or water.*"

In these proverbs we may perhaps see the differences between the European and the Greek proverb which Krumbacher and Hesseling have pointed out.[2] These differences lie in the form rather than in the content. In Western Europe popular wisdom sums up the situation in a general, didactic observation, while the Eastern proverb often shows a liking for a more concrete form. On the one hand we have a

---

1 Le Roux de Lincy, I, 139.
2 Krumbacher, "Mittelgriechische Sprichwörter," *Sitzungsberichte der Münchner Akademie, Phil.-Hist. Klasse,* 1893, II, No. 1; Hesseling, "Grieksche en Nederlandsche Spreekwoorden," *De Gids,* LXVI, pt. 4 (1902), 89–108 (reprinted in *Uit Byzantium en Hellas* [1911], pp. 169–195).

maxim and on the other an anecdote. The international proverb *Don't look a gift horse in the mouth* will serve as an illustration. The modern Greek version, which may stand for the Levantine forms generally, is *A man gave another an ass and he looked at its teeth* (Κάποιου χάριζαν γομάρι καὶ τὸ τήραε 's τὰ δόντια).[1] As Krumbacher, who cites the Greek proverb, points out, this difference enables us to distinguish the Western and Eastern forms of the proverb in Greece and thus to recognize the infiltration of Western tradition. In German the proverb *Out of the rain into the drip* (Aus dem Regen in die Traufe) expresses much the same idea as our *Out of the frying pan into the fire*; the Arabs put it in narrative form: *He fled the rain and went to sit under the drip of the gutter.* Cervantes uses a familiar proverb in this narrative form: *Said the pot to the kettle, "Get away, blackface"* (Digo la sarten á la caldera, quitate alla ojnegra, *Don Quijote*, ii, ch. lxvii). To this the Arabic parallel is *The kettle reproached the kitchen spoon. "Thou blackee,"* he said, *"thou idle babbler,"* and Abraham à Sancta Clara knew a similar version. And we may also compare the little known English proverb: *The raven said to the rook, "Stand away, black coat."*

The difference is striking, but it is by no means so generally true as these illustrations might lead us to think; the great majority of Greek and Arabic

---

1 Krumbacher, *Sitzungsberichte der Münchner Akademie, Phil.-Hist. Klasse*, 1893, II, 23.

proverbs resemble in form those current in Europe.[1] Hesseling is inclined to believe that the proverbs in the form of a dramatic dialogue are especially characteristic of Greek tradition; but it is rather a Levantine peculiarity of unknown origin. A more exhaustive description of such proverbs might throw light on questions of origin and style.

Epigrammatic Proverbs

The structure of proverbs is simple or complex. The great majority of proverbs make only a single assertion, although this assertion may be made regarding a combination of things and may not apply to them separately, e. g. *To promise and give nothing is comfort for a fool.* Such proverbs with compound subjects are not particularly frequent in English and German.[2] A more interesting class is that in which the same quality is assigned to two disparate objects, e. g. *A groaning horse and a groaning wife never fail their master*; *Children and fools speak the truth*; *Time and tide wait for no man.* The whimsical union of objects which have no relation at first sight imprints the proverb more deeply on our minds. Some prov-

1 Hesseling errs, I believe, in comparing such proverbs as "*Everything in measure," said the tailor, and beat his wife with the yardstick* ("Alles met mate," zei de kleermaker, en hij sloeg zijn vrouw met de el); see *De Gids*, LXVI, pt. 4 (1902), 94. Such proverbs will be discussed later as Wellerisms. I do not see the resemblance to the Eastern form. He explains the Eastern proverbs as condensed narratives, but the process is more or less doubtful since the narratives are not cited.
2 See Seiler, *Deutsche Sprichwörterkunde*, p. 222.

erbs of this sort have no doubt originated from natural causes. Others, which approach more nearly
the epigram, are recognizably foreign in origin and
have never become truly popular, e. g. *England is the
paradise of women, hell of horses, and purgatory of
servants*. It is probably safe to say that when the
proverb begins with an indication of the number of
members involved, as in *Three things drive a man out
of the house: smoke, rain, and a scolding wife*, it is foreign in origin or made on a foreign model; this special
form I shall discuss at length. Although sporadic
examples are found in the Middle Ages, epigrammatic
characterizations seem to have become the fashion
after the Renaissance and seem to have spread from
Italy. A careful examination of the history of this
fashion would be interesting and profitable.

Seiler was the first to recognize as a special group
those epigrammatic proverbs which are composed
of several members with specific indication of their
number.[1] An old and famous example of the type is
*Three things drive a man out of his house: smoke, rain,
and a scolding wife*. Seiler makes it clear that the type
began as an imitation of the Biblical "There be three
things" (Tria sunt . . ., *Prov.* xxx, 15, 18, 21, 29;
Ecclus. xxv, 9). Although the first indications of the
form are found in the Middle Ages, its greatest popularity came in the sixteenth century. At that time
proverbs which we know to have existed earlier in

1 *Deutsche Sprichwörterkunde*, pp. 222 ff.

other shapes were recast in this mould. In general, the form remained an artificial one which could not establish itself firmly in oral tradition. Two instances from oral tradition are: *There be three things that never comes to no good: Christmas pigs, Michaelmas fowls, and parsons' daughters* and *Three things are thrown away in a bowling green, namely, time, money, and oaths*, which Sir Walter Scott mentions in *The Fortunes of Nigel*, ch. xii.

A later development, which was also suggested directly by the Biblical model, is the mention of a fourth member, e. g.

> A smoke, a storme, and a contentious wife,
> Thre ils are found, that tire a husband's life:
> To which a fourth is by the proverb sed,
> When children cry for hunger, wanting bread.

Although the model lay ready to hand in "There be three things which are too wonderful for me, yea, four which I know not" (Tria sunt difficilia mihi et quattuor penitus ignoro, *Prov*. xxx, 18), it was not widely used. So far as my observation goes, this expanded form seems to have been employed almost exclusively in Germany and the adjoining Germanic countries. The English example which I have quoted seems to go back to a German source. In the *Figure of Foure* (1636, reprinted in 1654), Nicolas Breton gives many instances of the expanded form, but it is not easy to guess how firmly it had established itself in oral tradition. Much the same may be said of the earlier, anonymous *Les quatre choses*, which may have been printed at Lyons about 1490, and of Orazio Riminaldo's little-known *Libro di quatro cose* of uncertain date.[1]

As I have said, the form is semi-literary and the proverbs cited from the sixteenth century hardly have the ring of oral tradition, e. g. *Three things are unsatiable, priests, monckes, and the sea* (A.D. 1560); *Three thinges a man lendeth rife, His horse, his fighting sword, his wife* (A.D. 1577). The German examples run into the hundreds,[2] but sound quite as artificial as the English. In the heyday of its popularity Ulrich von Hutten wrote a bitter satire on Papal Rome entitled *Trias Romana* (1520) which betokens the currency of the form. Another scrap of evidence which shows how the form struggled to establish itself is seen in the conversion of a fable into a proverb of this type: *In their behavior three things are more steadfast than others: suspicion, the wind, and loyalty; the first never leaves a place it has entered; the second never enters when it cannot see a way of escape; the third never returns to a place it has left* (Tre cose inanimate sono più ferme che l'altre nel loro uso: il sospetto, il vento e la lealtà; il primo mai non entra in luogo, donde poi si parta, l'altro mai non entra, d'onde non vegga l'uscita, l'altra, d'onde un tratto si parte, mai non vi ritorna).[3]

1 See Bonser, *Proverb Literature* (London, 1930), p. 131, No. 1093, and p. 273, No. 2237.
2 See Wander, *Deutsches Sprichwörter-lexikon, s. v.* Drei.
3 Wesselski, *Poliziano*, p. 232, No. 403.

It does not seem to be possible to trace this saying beyond a fable of Petrarch's in which fire, wind, water, and suspicion travel together and on taking leave of one another give signs by which they may be recognized.

Probably the most popular of all proverbs in this form is *Three things drive a man out of his house: smoke, rain, and a scolding wife.* A brief review of its history will be illuminating. The germ from which it sprang is the Biblical "A continual dropping in a very rainy day and a contentious woman are alike" (Tecta perstillantia in die frigoris et litigiosa mulier comparantur, *Prov.* xxvii, 15), which Pope Innocent III remoulded into "Tria sunt quae non sinunt hominem in domo permanere: fumus, stillicidium et mala uxor." No doubt he recalled an allegorical interpretation by Petrus Cantor. The actual words of Solomon could not establish themselves in tradition, while Pope Innocent's version was taken up by the *Facetus*, a handbook of admonitions regarding manners and morals, the *Dialogue of Solomon and Marcolf*, a rude satirical dispute between a wise man and a fool, and the Goliardic *De conjuge non ducenda.* Although these works belong to the lower levels of literature, they were very widely disseminated in the Middle Ages. Chaucer took our proverb into the *Tale of Melibeus* from the moralizing of Albertanus of Brescia. So general an acceptance of the proverb and so wide a publication ensured its general adoption: we find it expanded into more than a thousand lines of mediaeval Latin verse, we find it in a Welsh wedding ceremony, in a shrove-tide play of Hans Sachs, and in a diatribe against immorality and corruption based on the legendary life of Judas (Abraham à Sancta Clara, *Judas der Ertz-Schelm* [1686]), and finally, much altered, in Shakespere's *1 Henry IV*. It also appears that the development of the formula *There are three evil things, . . . and the fourth is . . .*, which we have already quoted, comes very late in the history of the proverb. Even this proverb, which had an unusually wide distribution early in the Middle Ages, does not seem to have left much mark on oral tradition; other proverbs which were less fortunate are preserved for us only by the collections of the seventeenth and eighteenth centuries.

NATIONAL AND RACIAL TRAITS

Many have sought to identify national or local traits in proverbs and to use them in describing and defining national or racial temperament. Perhaps no side of proverbial study has been prosecuted so long and so vigorously, but the results are insignificant.[1]

---

1 See such essays as Kradolfer, "Das Italienische Sprichwort und seine Beziehungen zum Deutschen," *Zeitschrift für Völkerpsychologie*, IX (1877), 185–271; Berneker, "Das Russische Volk in seinen Sprichwörtern," *Zeitschrift des Vereins für Volkskunde*, XIV (1904), 75–87, 179–191; N. Gerbel, "Nationale Sprüchwörter der Franzosen," *Das Ausland*, XLIII (1870), 93–95; XLIV (1871), 226–229; V. Granlund, "Svenska Folket i sina Ordspråk," *Svenska Fornminnesföreningens Tidskrift*, I (1871), 27–45.

All the endeavors are fruitless and unavailing. Before they are likely to attain useful results we must have exhaustive studies of the history and distribution of individual proverbs. A few proverbs can be recognized as regional, e. g. *Day follows even on the winter night* (Dag följer även på vinternatten); *A life without love, a year without summer* (Ett liv utan kärlek, ett år utan sommar); *The sun shines even into a little room* (Solen skiner också på liten stuga); *Midsummer night is not long, but it sets many cradles rocking* (Midsommarnatten är icke lång, men den sätter många vaggor i gång) [1] are from the far North. Archbishop Trench says that *Make hay while the sun shines* is truly English. After all, the gain from collecting such proverbs, when they can be recognized, is likely to be slight. We must not put much reliance in such assertions as that *Love me little, love me long* is a Southern and not a Scandinavian proverb. We can put no reliance in them when they are not based on detailed investigations of history and dissemination. *The Devil is not as black as he is painted*, when it is found in Swedish, does not prove that the trait of justice, even to the most undeserving, is typically Swedish.

Essays on the national traits exhibited in proverbs give abundant evidence that their authors found examples to support preconceived notions. Few of these essays determine their objectives and the means to

1 Ström, *Svenskarna i sina Ordspråk* (Stockholm, 1926), pp. 307, 38, 62, 34.

attain them. It would seem obvious that the deductions which can be made from proverbs with international distribution are different from the deductions
which can be made from a proverb restricted to a
single country or province. Ordinarily these essays
do not set out to discover new facts. Perhaps the observation that ancient Greek proverbs contain many
allusions to mythology is significant: the contrast
with the sobriety and practical sense of Roman proverbs seems to give it force and meaning.[1] The Cas-
tilian *pundonor* is surely to be found in Spanish proverbs by one who looks for it. The employment of
proverbs to determine characteristic or essential racial
traits is neither the easiest nor the most reliable means
of defining qualities so difficult to appraise. If proverbs are to be used, it is very likely that the estimates
recorded in the traditional comment of neighboring
peoples would throw light in dark corners.

Long ago Francis Bacon said, "The genius, wit,
and spirit of a nation are discovered in its proverbs,"
and many have repeated it after him. But proverbs
which are international in their currency can scarcely
reveal and illuminate national traits unless we argue
that the acceptance of a bit of international property
constitutes in itself a defining of national characteristics. We should know, moreover, that we are dealing
with an international proverb before we use it as evi-

[1] Otto "Die Götter und Halbgötter im [Lateinischen] Sprichwort,"
Archiv für Lateinische Lexikographie, III (1886), 207–229, 384–387.

dence. We must also reckon with a large stock of proverbs resting on fundamental human traits which transcend the national. It might seem that Erasmus was asserting the contrary when he compared proverbs to wines which cannot be transported out of the land in which they have grown. It is apparent, however, that we cannot make much use of the fact that proverbs possess peculiarities which bind them to the soil until we know what those peculiarities are. The first step is obviously a minute examination of each individual proverb or formula. With a large number of special studies in hand, we may hope to draw some general conclusions of value, and we may ultimately be able to define a specifically German and a specifically French group of proverbs; but even when we have done so, it may turn out that the two groups do not show striking or significant psychological and stylistic differences. If the aim of our studies is to discover such differences, the game is scarcely worth the candle.

Perhaps we may see exemplified in proverbs a difference between the spirit of one epoch and that of another, but again we are likely to find the results for which we are looking rather than results based on objective facts. On the whole, the differences in proverbs of various ages seem somewhat easier to discover than do the differences in proverbs of different countries. Certainly the collection of the materials and the presuppositions are less difficult and compli-

cated. Yet it is interesting to observe that there have
been few attempts to find strata of different ages in
the proverbs of any country. In contrast to the
more recent Germanic proverbs, Heusler [1] characterizes the Old Germanic proverb as calm, confident,
manly, and distrustful. Fate dominates its ethical
ideas. The rare flashes of humor are not kindly.
Modern sayings, he believes, turn on simple, everyday
events and show a hesitant, renunciatory mood
mingled with kindliness and whimsicality. It would
be interesting to notice whether contradictory proverbs belong to different cultural epochs or whether,
as has been suggested, they only mark out the middle
way. The difference between the older and newer
strata of Germanic proverbs has been brought about,
Heusler believes, by the passing of the viking spirit
and by the handing on to the common man of the
fashion of proverb-making. It exemplifies what hap-
pens when a literary fashion or artistic device passes
from higher to lower levels of society.

ETHICAL TRAITS

The most striking trait in the ethics of proverbs is
the adherence to the middle way, and indeed their
reason for existence lies in that fact. Proverbs will not
champion martyrdom or villainy, although *I'll try
anything once* and *You never miss a slice from a cut loaf*
have no doubt brought much misery in their train.

1 *Altgermanische Dichtung* (Handbuch der Literaturwissenschaft), p. 68.

Just as reflective men see life in the light of eternal truths and formulate them in apothegms and aphorisms, so the folk seeks and finds support in the common humanity of proverbial philosophy. It is perhaps a poor sort of consolation to say *It will be all the same in a hundred years*; *Misfortunes never come singly*; *It will all come out in the wash*; *Be good and you'll be happy*, or, with whimsical irony, *The worst is yet to come* and *You can't keep a good man down*, but life has little more encouragement for the ordinary man and the thought has served the needs of simple folk. Of course the middle way is marked on both sides by contradictions. A sound skepticism pervades proverbial wisdom and ventures to show itself in assertions which no member of the folk would dare utter as his own. Formal doctrine receives short shrift, but God is treated with respect. Empty show is condemned, even though proverbs recognize that it often wins success. A more detailed illustration of such contradictions is unnecessary, and the labor of assembling them may satisfy antiquarian curiosity, but it is not likely to yield useful results.

Obscene Proverbs

Sayings offensive to good manners are comparatively rare, although we must recognize that taste alters with the passage of time. Many proverbs which seem inelegant today once offended no one. Ray puts the situation briefly in the preface to the second edition of *A Collection of English Proverbs* (1678): "But though I do condemn the mention of anything obscene, yet I cannot think all use of slovenly and dirty words to be such a violation of modesty, as to exact the discarding all Proverbs of which they are ingredients. The useful notions which many ill-worded Proverbs do import, may, I think, compensate for their homely terms; though I could wish the contrivers of them had put their sense into more decent and cleanly language." Alterations in taste in language are difficult to discover; and it is even more difficult to know how significant they are as indications of tendencies in manners. So far as inferences regarding the course of manners are permissible, offensive words tend to disappear from proverbs. The vulgar metaphor does not long maintain itself. Of course, the folk does not display a fastidious taste in choosing materials and metaphors, but there are, I believe, signs that a purificatory process goes on in tradition. Apparently the contraction *Peor es meneallo* ('It is worse to stir it') is created to avoid a vulgar word and *One ill weed marreth a whole pot of pottage* has variants of a more offensive form. *The pot calls the kettle black* and the proverbial phrase *To sit* (var. *fall*) *between two stools* exist in older and well-established versions, which may even be original; they were evidently an offense to good taste.

We really know very little about outspokenly obscene and erotic proverbs. The collections which exist seem to be more concerned with preserving offensive materials than with selecting traditional proverbs. It is hard to estimate the number, distribution, and importance of such proverbs. Two kinds are to be distinguished: superstitions which have in some way acquired a fixed form and proverbs which make some ethical or moral observation regarding appetites or passions, e. g. *P. erectus non habet conscientiam* or a variant form made on the model of *Necessity knows no law*. Obscene proverbial superstitions, which have already been discussed under the head of health proverbs, deal chiefly with comparisons of the proportions of different parts of the body. As in all traditional material, we must expect to find a good deal about simple functions in proverbs. Of course proverbs dealing with these matters are likely to escape print, but that is no argument for their non-existence.[1] Although we cannot examine the subject further here, the old saw *Naturalia non sunt turpia* ('What is natural is not vile') finds appropriate application.

PROVERBS AND LITERATURE

In works of literature the use of proverbs varies in manner and degree from age to age. At all times proverbs have meant more to the folk than to the learned. Erasmus speaks as a scholar and conscious

1 The collections printed in *Kryptadia* and *Anthropophyteia* offer little enough of value; I have not troubled to run down the *Bibliotheca Scatologica* cited in the Bernstein catalogue, No. 294. See Kainis, *Die Derbheiten im Reden des Volkes* (Leipzig, n.d.).

literary artist when he calls proverbs "condimenta" which must be used intelligently when one writes or speaks. Proverbs are used freely in writings which make an appeal to the folk and in those in which the folk is characterized; in those classes of literature which are far removed from the folk, proverbs rarely occur. We see these distinctions already in classical writers: Aristophanes, Theophrastus, Lucian, and Plautus use proverbs easily and naturally. Writings which make a conspicuous effort at literary style generally avoid them except as details characterizing the folk. Our Saviour quotes proverbs readily, and the Church Fathers use them in writings with a popular appeal. Throughout the Middle Ages proverbs were frequently used in literature, and individual preferences manifested themselves then as now. The German court epic, which is a relatively artificial and cultured product, shows a disinclination for them; writings nearer to the folk use them freely. Yet we must not carry these distinctions too far: Chaucer's *Troilus*, a very sophisticated, anti-popular poem, bristles with proverbs. Didactic writers naturally show a great liking for proverbs. A satirical tone and an appeal to fundamental emotions encourage the use of proverbs. A proverb is often a ready-made epigram, sums up the situation effectively, drives home the point, and appeals to the reader's or hearer's sense of humor. Consequently proverbs are much used in ages of controversy and satirical criticism: the German and Latin literature of the Reformation abound in them.

In later literary history we do not see any significant variations in these fundamental ways of using proverbs. Calderon, on the one hand, eschews them and Lope de Vega, on the other, quotes them freely. This variation reflects the essential difference of the two dramatists. Cervantes characterizes Sancho Panza by the ease with which proverbs drop from his lips, and similarly Shakespere puts the proverb in the mouth of the folk. It becomes a mannerism in the figure of Nicholas Proverbs in Henry Porter's *Two Angry Women of Abingdon*. These differences persist: Dickens uses proverbs more easily and naturally than Thackeray.

We can observe different attitudes toward proverbs in different ages. Before the *Collectanea Adagiorum* (1500) of Erasmus the attitude was primarily one of didacticism. In the beginning and among savage peoples proverbs often have religious associations, and later they find a place in the schoolroom. Then Erasmus aroused an interest in the proverb for its own sake, and for the next two centuries proverbs were translated from one language into another, huge collections were assembled, and dissertations of all kinds were written about them. During the eighteenth century a reaction set in: the rationalistic temper found little to admire in proverbs. Finally, a new interest sprang up in the nineteenth century along with nationalistic or racial strivings and the awakening interest in the folk and its ways of self-expression.

We must also mention those literary works in which the interest in proverbs is of primary, not subsidiary, importance. In early times proverbs were collected for their didactic value, as rules and guides for life. Such collections in the Old Testament, Old English, and Icelandic pass as literary monuments and not as mere assemblings of proverbial material. So similar are the proverbs and the incidental editorial comment that we cannot always separate them. The Middle Ages used proverbs in instruction in foreign languages and rhetoric, and although Humanism and the Renaissance cast aside the collections on which such exercises were based, the method still persists. Text-books in foreign languages often include proverbs, and the German school-boy still writes themes based on proverbs. After mentioning some efforts to invent proverbs we shall return to certain closely allied literary forms.

A curious accompaniment of long familiarity with proverbs often appears in the belief that new proverbs can be invented. Intimate acquaintance with the manner of proverbs awakens confidence in the ability to create others. In almost every case the results have given the lie to the belief. James Howell, who in 1659 published the first very large English collection, ventured to compose "Divers centuries of new sayings,

which may serve for proverbs to posterity." Not one
of them has, I dare say, found a place in oral or even
learned tradition. It would perhaps be difficult to say
just why the vital spark is lacking, but its absence is
beyond question. Benjamin Franklin may have hit
the popular vein more successfully with the aphorisms
in *Poor Richard's Almanac* (1732–1758), but even of
these only a few have survived in oral tradition, e. g.
A penny saved is a penny earned; and this proverb,
which was already known in the sixteenth century,
owes its form and not its thought to him. Perhaps
we can credit Franklin with the invention of *Three
removes are worse than a fire*. We must remember that Franklin drew freely on Ray's collection
(1670) and such others as were available to him. At
the beginning of his literary career K. F. W. Wander,
the compiler of a huge lexicon of German proverbs,
issued several volumes of original proverbs which
died still-born: *Scheidemünze, ein Taschenbuch für
Jedermann, Oder: 5000 Neue Deutsche Sprichwörter*
(1831), and a second volume of the same work, which
appeared in 1835 along with *Nüsse für Kinder aufs
Ganze Jahr Oder Turnübungen für Verstand, Scharf-
sinn und Witz, in einer Sammlung Neuer Sprichwörter*.
As a matter of fact, Wander's inventing of proverbs
has cast some suspicion on his lexicon, for he does not
always give sources for his quotations. Many proverbs which are not supported by quotations seem to
be his translations from other languages; perhaps he

thought that tradition would make them its own. Alexander F. Chamberlain, long the editor of the *Journal of American Folk-lore*, collected and invented maxims suggested by modern life and science in the hope that one or another might become proverbial; but his efforts are not notably successful.[1] The "literary" proverb, if one can speak of such a thing, is a dreary chapter in both literary and proverbial history.

On a somewhat higher artistic plane we find collections of aphorisms and emblems. Although these do not pass themselves off as actual proverbs, they employ more or less closely the form and subject-matter of proverbs. The rise of emblem-books and their age of popularity agree with the rise and popularity of proverb collections. After the Renaissance, collections of engravings with accompanying inscriptions in prose or verse became very popular. In many instances one finds it hard to say whether the engraving illustrates the inscription or the inscription explains the engraving. The model for later collections was Andrea Alciati's *Emblemata* (first complete ed. 1551). Emblem-books were especially favored by the Dutch; some of the greatest Dutch poets of the seventeenth century composed them. Proverbs were used to some extent in emblem-books, and the subject-matter and the aphoristic view of the world have much in common with the temper of proverbs. Compositions in the

1 "Proverbs in the Making: Some Scientific Commonplaces," *Journal of American Folk-lore*, XVII (1904), 161–170, 268–278.

proverbial vein are not infrequent. Goethe set his aphorisms apart in his works under the caption "Sprichwörtliches"; presumably he regarded them as efforts in the proverbial manner. The same may be said of Edward Fitzgerald's *Polonius*. More ambitious endeavors in the same direction are Martin Tupper's *Proverbial Philosophy*, a book which summed up the sententious observations and notions of the middle of the last century, or the writings of such men as J. F. Castelli and J. N. Vogl of Vienna in the first half of the century. Such compositions are unendurably dull today.

It is not surprising that the most interesting and important literary monument associated with proverbs should bear the name of Solomon. The Old Testament collects his wise sayings, many of which have found new currency in the oral tradition of Western Europe. Legend associates with Solomon stories of a combat of wits in which his opponent was the Queen of Sheba, Hiram of Tyre, or another less familiar figure. Although the early development of this legend is extremely obscure, we find it widely known in the Middle Ages. From almost the beginning of its history the legend is separated into two branches, one predominantly narrative and the other predominantly proverbial in subject and treatment. With the narrative branch we need not concern ourselves further, although its complicated and extensive history needs elucidation. In the proverbial branch we see a

definite trend from the serious to the comic and obscene. The Old English *Salomon and Saturnus* is a
sober disputation on religious matters. In the course
of time, Solomon's opponent becomes his foil and is
degraded to a jester who stops at nothing. In the mediaeval dialogue of Solomon and Marcolf the shrewd,
witty, and vulgar fool caps each wise saying of Solomon's with an obscene proverb or parody. Almost
every country in Europe possessed translations of
this dialogue. Special developments in French are
dialogues which have become almost entirely obscene. Although the full history of this transformation of the Biblical Solomon and the legends about
him can never be written, the main outlines of the
deterioration are clear.[1]

We have already noticed the tendency of proverbs
to form models for the invention of parallel proverbs.
In some instances these parallel proverbs exist in con-
junction with the original proverb. Thus the saying
Praise the fair day at even probably began as a simple
assertion, but it is often found in compound form:
*Schöne Tage soll man abends loben, schöne Frauen mor-
gens* ('One should praise beautiful days in the evening, beautiful women in the morning'); *Sed vero laus*

1 See J. M. Kemble, *The Dialogue of Salomon and Saturnus* (Ælfric
Society, London, 1848); F. Vogt, *Salman und Morolf* (Halle, 1880);
A. Ritter von Vincenti, *Die Altenglischen Dialoge von Salomon und
Saturn* (*Münchener Beiträge*, XXXI), 1904; W. Benary, *Salomon et
Marcolfus* (Sammlung Mittellateinischer Texte, VIII [Heidelberg,
1914]).

in fine canitur, et vespere laudatur dies ('But, truly, praise should be sung at the end, and the day should be praised in the evening'); *Vespere laudatur lux, hospes mane probatur* ('The light should be praised in the evening; the host is tested on the morrow'). In fact, the oldest instance of the proverb in a Germanic language occurs in a series:

> At kveldi skal dag leyfa, kono, er brend er,
> mæki, er reyndr er, mey, er gefin er,
> ís, er yfir kømr, ǫl, er drukkit er.

> ('Praise the day at even, a wife when dead,
> a weapon when tried, a maid when married,
> ice when 'tis crossed, and ale when 'tis drunk.')
> *Hávamál*, 81.

This listing resembles a curious literary form, the Priamel, which enjoyed remarkable literary vogue in Germany during the fifteenth century and a little later. The exact nature of this literary form is difficult to define: it consisted in an accumulation of assertions, usually unrelated in appearance, which are often united at the end by a single remark binding them together in an epigram.[1] Since the form is so indeterminate, scholars have sought and found its origins in many other ages and countries. Indeed the similarity of the Old Norse verses which have just been quoted to some Finnish verses on the one hand and to some Sanskrit epigrams on the other have led

---

1 See Euling, "Priamel," *Reallexikon der Deutschen Literaturgeschichte*, II (1926–28), 723–725.

Comparetti and others to declare that these are relics of an ancient verse-form.[1] The Finnish verses are

> Praise your new horse in the morning,
> Your wife in the second year,
> Only in the third year your brother-in-law,
> And yourself never in your life,

and the Sanskrit epigram is "Praise food when it is digested; the wife, when her youth is past; the hero, when he has returned from battle; the grain, when it is harvested." Whether we can safely make such an excursion as this into literary prehistory must remain more than doubtful.

In essence the Priamel is an epigrammatic improvisation which uses proverbs in part. If we conceive the form so simply, — and it is difficult to make a better working definition, — it has existed from time immemorial and is closely allied to all early aphoristic writing. Even in the fifteenth century, when the Priamel flourished in the hands of Hans Rosenplüt, a Meistersinger of Nuremberg, it failed to establish itself as a distinct and permanent literary form. Apparently it stood so close to improvisation that it was unable to separate itself. In this way the literary form which most nearly expressed the genius of the proverb failed to come to full realization.

An interesting use of proverbs appears in *La*

1 R. M. Meyer, *Die Altgermanische Poesie* (Berlin, 1889), p. 434 (quoting H. Paul, *Kanteletar*, p. 143); Heusler, *Zeitschrift des Vereins für Volkskunde*, XXVI (1916), 43.

Comédie des Proverbes, which is ordinarily ascribed to Adrien de Montluc, Comte de Cramail. It is variously dated between 1609 and 1632. In the simplest and most conventional sort of plot, the author inserts all the proverbs at his command. With surprising wit and ingenuity he fits the proverbs to the situation. The comedy was translated as the Zugabe to the second volume of G. P. Harsdörffer's *Frauenzimmer- gesprächspiele* (2d ed., 1644). It seems to follow the traditions of French and Italian farce, closer to the former in style, to the latter in characters and plot. Why the author hit upon the trick of using proverbs so freely remains uncertain. Even earlier than Mont- luc's comedy is the anonymous dialogue, *Les Menus Propos*, of the end of the fifteenth century.[1] Cer- vantes wrote a similar composition, *El Entremés de Refranes*. There is enough plain speech to give the thread of the story, but proverbs are quoted wherever possible. According to Tuinman,[2] the Dutch drama- tist Paffenrode (1618–1673) wrote a dialogue in prov- erbs, but I have not found it in his *Gedigten* (Am- sterdam, 1711). A prose example of the same sort, Francisco de Quevedo Villegas's *Cuento de Cuentos*, tells of a family quarrel involving an unruly daughter and her lover. A somewhat similar device is seen in the figure of Nicholas Proverbs in Henry Porter's *Two Angry Women of Abingdon* (1598). From painting I

---

1 See Bonser, *Proverb Literature* (London, 1930), p. 127, Nos. 1059, 1060.
2 *De Oorsprong en Uitlegging van Dagelyks Gebruikte Nederduitsche Spreekwoorden*, Eerste Voorrede, p. [vii].

might call to mind the parallel in Pieter Breughel's marvelously ingenious and dramatic assembling of more than a hundred proverbs on a single canvas.[1] Small collections of proverbs, farragoes without a thread of dramatic or narrative interest to hold them together, are often used to gain more or less successfully a particular effect. To this end François Villon wrote a "Ballade en Proverbes,"[2] John Heywood composed *A Dialogue Conteyning the Number of the Effectuall Prouerbes in the English Tonge, Compact in a Matter Concernynge two Maner of Mariages* (1562), Jean Antoine de Baïf wrote four books of sestets (*Les Mimes, Enseignements et Proverbes* [1581]), Rabelais (*Pantagruel,* V, ch. xxii) described the "Proverb Island,"[3] the sixteenth-century *Faustbuch* devoted a chapter to proverbs,[4] and Carl Sandburg heaps them up in "Good Morning, America."

Another dramatic use of proverbs is found in the *proverbes dramatiques*, so widely known in the latter half of the eighteenth century. In these plays, which are something after the manner of a charade, the audience is led by degrees to guess the proverb on

1 See W. Fraenger, *Der Bauern-Bruegel und das deutsche Sprichwort* (Erlenbach-Zürich, n.d. [1923]). G. P. C. van Breugel, *Gedenkschrift wegens een Schilderij van Spreekwoorden* (Haarlem, 1876), seems to have been overlooked by later writers.
2 Conveniently reprinted in Duplessis, *Bibliographie Parémiologique* (Paris, 1847), p. 125.
3 See Fraenger, as above, pp. 11 ff.
4 See Fränkel and Bauer, "Entlehnungen in ältesten Faustbuch. 1. Das Sprichwörterkapitel," *Vierteljahrschrift für Litteraturgeschichte,* IV, (1891), 361–381.

which the play depends for its point and purpose. Ordinarily the invention of this sort of play is credited to Carmontelle (1717–1806), but Leroux de Lincy (I, p. lxxx) asserts that its beginnings reach back into the seventeenth century, when Mme. de Maintenon wrote no less than thirty-nine such plays. There seems to be more or less question about the plays of Mme. de Maintenon, and certainly the first author who made a name in the genre was Carmontelle. Similar plays began to be written in the latter part of the eighteenth century; and in the nineteenth, Théodore le Clercq, Alfred de Musset, and Octave Feuillet continued the tradition. The German imitations, e. g. M. G. Saphir, *Narreteisprichwörter*, which I have been unable to see; C. J. Pulvermacher, *Taschenbuch Dramatischer Sprichwörter* (Berlin, 1835); C. E. von Benzel-Sternau, *Das Hoftheater von Barataria* (Leipzig, 1828); Luise Hölder, *Dramatische Sprichwörter zur Schauspielmässigen Darstellung* (Munich, 1838), never attained an equal level of literary importance. After all, we are very ill informed regarding the history and nature of this minor literary genre.[1]

---

1 See R. Werner, *Zur Geschichte der "Proverbes Dramatiques"* (Berlin, 1887), and Deiardin, *Dictionnaire des Spots ou Proverbs Wallons* (Liège, 1863), p. 37. I have not seen P. R. Faiex, *La Chasse aux Proverbes* (n. p., n. d.), which is cited in the Bernstein catalogue, No. 1073.

IV

PROVERBIAL PHRASES, WELLERISMS, AND PROVERBIAL COMPARISONS

PROVERBIAL PHRASES [1]

THE proverbial phrase exhibits the characteristic rigidity of the proverb in all particulars except grammatical form. A proverb does not vary in any regard, while a proverbial phrase shifts according to time and person. *He pulls the chestnuts out of the fire* may vary according to tense and subject. In general, the problems which arise in connection with the proverbial phrase are the same as for the proverb. Interest turns chiefly on the history and dissemination of individual phrases and on their origin and meaning. It is

[1] Although many collections make no sharp distinction between proverbs and proverbial phrases, the latter are generally more difficult to collect. The best annotated collections are Dutch, and are valuable for any European language because of the international distribution of the more important and interesting proverbial phrases. Significant collections of proverbial phrases are Hyamson, *A Dictionary of English Phrases* (London, 1922); de Cock, *Spreekwoorden en Zegswijzen, Afkomstig van Oude Gebruiken* (Ghent, 1905, 1908), *Spreekwoorden en Zegswijzen over de Vrouwen, de Liefde en het Huwelijk* (Ghent, 1911), and *Spreekwoorden en Zegswijzen op Volksgeloof Berustend* (Ghent, 1919); Stoett, *Nederlandsche Spreekwoorden, Spreekwijzen, Uitdrukkingen en Gezegden* (Zutphen, 1923–25); Borchardt-Wustmann, *Die Sprichwörtlichen Redensarten im Deutschen Volksmund nach Sinn and Ursprung Erläutert* (Leipzig, 6th ed., 1925); Richter, *Deutsche Redensarten* (Leipzig, 4th ed., 1921); Schrader, *Der Bilderschmuck der Deutschen*

ordinarily more difficult to trace the history of a proverbial phrase than of a proverb, since the sources are
very hard to assemble. Older collections of proverbs
only occasionally include proverbial phrases; dictionaries mention them infrequently and carelessly;
and even modern collections of proverbs often show
equally little interest in them.

Many proverbial phrases can boast of a very long
and respectable history. Some which have a surprisingly modern and popular ring are first mentioned in
the Latin and Greek classics: *to open his eyes* [to a
situation]; *to be as hungry as a bear*; *to touch a sore
spot*; *to have eyes in the back of his head*; *to be full of
vinegar*, i. e. 'to be high-spirited.' Aristophanes used
the phrase *to quarrel over the ass's shadow* (*Wasps*,
l. 191), and it is still current in Italy.[1] Biblical sources
gave their share: *to be a thorn in the flesh* (Lanceae in
lateribus, *Num.* xxx, 55); *to build on sand* (Similis erit
viro stulto, qui aedificavit domum suam super are-

Sprache (Weimar, 6th ed., 1901); Otto, *Die Sprichwörter und Sprichwörtlichen Redensarten der Römer* (Leipzig, 1890); Caballero, *Dic-
cionario de Modismos* (*Frases y Metáforas*) (Madrid, 1905). Wander
(*Deutsches Sprichwörter-Lexikon*) gives many German proverbial
phrases and distinguishes them with a star. A great deal of information
about the proverbial phrases is available in *Notes and Queries* (London),
but the lack of a cumulative index makes reference difficult. Com-
prehensive studies, e. g. L. P. Smith, *Words and Idioms: Studies in the
English Language* (Boston, 1925), and W. Gottschalk, *Die Sprichwörtlichen Redensarten der französischen Sprache* (Heidelberg, 1930), are
rare.

1 Seiler, *Die Entwicklung der Deutschen Kultur im Spiegel des Deutschen Lehnworts*, V [Halle, 1921], *Das Deutsche Lehnsprichwort*, Pt. I,
p. 125.

nam, *Matt.* vii, 26); *to wash one's hands of a thing* (Lavi inter innocentes manus meas, *Ps.* lxxii, 13); *to heap coals of fire on his head* (Carbones ignis congeres super caput eius, *Rom.* xii, 20). Especially interesting are the fortunes of *to cast pearls before swine* (Neque mittatis margaritas vestras ante porcos, *Matt.* vii, 6), which is the source of the Dutch *to scatter roses before swine* (Roozen strooien voor de varkens). Very probably we have a confusion of Latin "margarita," 'pearl' and French "marguérite," 'daisy, flower.' St. Jerome appears to be responsible for *to make a virtue of necessity.* Seneca knew the saying *to sit between two stools.* Allusions to Aesopic fables are frequent: *to burst with envy*; *to blow hot and cold*; *to get the lion's share*; and to other classical stories, e. g. *to hang by a thread.* Although the English phrase *to cut the Gordian knot* has lost the original idiom, which is preserved in the German *den gordischen Knoten lösen* ('to loosen or untie the Gordian knot'), it gives us a better and clearer picture.

Many proverbial phrases are international in their currency, and for this reason the excellent Dutch and German treatises on proverbial phrases are often very useful in studying English or American turns of speech. Typical international proverbial phrases are: *to get out of bed with the wrong foot first*; *to break the ice,* i. e. 'to overcome a social stiffness'; *to jump from the frying pan into the fire*; *to hear the grass grow*; *to put* (var. *set, harness*) *the cart before the horse.* It is inter-

esting to note the variations in *to buy a pig in a poke*.
The earliest forms, which were already current in the
Middle Ages, speak merely of "buying in a sack,"
i. e. 'buying sight unseen,' as in

> Swer inme sack koufet,
> und sich mit tôren roufet,
> und borget ungewisser diet,
> der singet dicke klageliet.

> ('Whoever buys in a sack,
> and quarrels with fools,
> and lends to unreliable people,
> often sings a song of sorrow.')
>
> Freidank, lxxxv, 5.

Luther still uses the mediaeval form. The cat, which
is of course a dishonest substitute for the hare, early
enters the phrase.[1] The pig, which is evidently a
sucking pig, appears in both English and German
forms from the seventeenth century on and is apparently the latest development.

The internationally used phrase *to sell the skin before you have caught the bear* goes back to a fable introduced into the Aesopic collections by Laurentius
Abstemius in 1495. Although several have seen in
this phrase the origin of the term "bear" for one who
sells shares of stock he does not possess, the explanation is scarcely to be accepted. A satisfactory explanation would account for "bull" at the same time.

Especial interest attaches to the origin and cultural

---

1 Compare "Bien lor savoit chat en sac vendre" (*Joufrois*, l. 1674).

background of proverbial phrases. Many phrases, to
be sure, offer nothing of interest, and once they are
pointed out as proverbial, can be passed over without more ado, e. g. *to wind him around your finger,
to pour out one's heart, to blow one's own horn, to be
tarred with the same stick, to build castles in Spain,*
which is first found in mediaeval French, *to be caught
red-handed, to set the North River* (var.: *Thames*) *on
fire.* Some phrases are amusing for their whimsicality: *to know which side his bread is buttered on; to look
as if butter would not melt in his mouth; to feel like
a fish out of water; to make two bites of a cherry* (said
of a fastidious person). These, like proverbs and proverbial phrases generally, involve a simple metaphor
which gives a scene a general instead of a specific
application.

A classification of the fields of human activity from
which tradition draws proverbial phrases is illuminating, although it is difficult in the absence of a good
English collection. What can be said here is only by
way of suggestion and owes much to the remarks of
L. P. Smith.[1] Mediaeval punishments evidently im-
printed themselves on popular fancy: *to curse with bell,
book, and candle; to put him on the rack; to run the
gauntlet; to put the screws on.* From the procedure of
canonization we have *to be the Devil's advocate* and *to
be on the side of the angels.* The phrase *to fly false*

1 *Words and Idioms: Studies in the English Language* (Boston, 1925),
ch. v.

colors suggests a piratical trick or a warlike stratagem, and the origin of *to walk the plank* is obvious. Many proverbial phrases are taken from card-playing: *to have an ace up his sleeve*; *to lay all the cards on the table*; *to stack the cards*; *to hold all the cards*; *to pass the buck* (the "buck" is any object used to designate the dealer, and as the deal passes from one player to another, the buck is passed); *to euchre*; *to stake everything on the turn of a card*; *to call his bluff*; *to trump his ace*. Others refer to gambling of different kinds and particularly to horse-racing: *to have little (nothing, everything) at stake*; *to be out of the running*; *to bet on the wrong horse*; *to be left at the post*; *to hold the whip-hand*; *to play with loaded dice*; *to stake everything on one throw*; *to bank on*; *to draw the short straw*. Many are derived from sports: *to be at fault* and *to be in at the death* (fox hunting); *to bark up the wrong tree* ('coon hunting); *to hold* (var. *run*) *with the hare and run* (var. *hunt*) *with the hounds*; *to draw a red herring across the trail*; *to beat about the bush*; *to fall into a trap*; *to have shot one's bolt*; *to have him in the nine hole* (billiards); *to have two strikes on him*; *to be caught with his foot off first base*. From boxing and wrestling we have *to be down but not out*; *to take the count*; *to give him a body blow*; *to hit below the belt*; *to have him on the hip*; *to throw up the sponge*. Cock fighting yields *to live like a fighting cock*; *to stand steel*; *to show the white feather*; and perhaps even *to turn tail*.

Proverbial phrases from seafaring life seem to be

more frequent proportionally than proverbs from the same source. Typical examples are: *to be in the same boat with, to steer clear of a thing, to put in an oar, to sail close to the wind, to pour oil on troubled waters,* and perhaps *to carry it through to the bitter end.* Many others owe their origin to military life: *to pass muster, to fall into line, to steal a march on a person, to stand one's ground, to bear the brunt of the attack.* Country life contributes a large share: *to kick over the traces, to put one's shoulder to the wheel, to feel his oats, to take the bull by the horns, to put a spoke in his wheel, to tar with the same brush, to go the whole hog, to feather one's nest, to clip his wings, to crow over, to pull in his horns,* i. e. 'to be less arrogant,' *to take to a thing like a duck to water, to lie fallow, to break fresh ground.* Others are taken from the household: *to lay on the shelf, to go like clockwork, to put the lid on, to stew in one's own juice, to have a finger in the pie, to be on pins and needles, to look for a needle in a haystack, to be at loose ends, to pin him down.* The phrase *to rule the roost* is really "to rule the roast." The trades and modern mechanical devices yield an abundance: *to put through the mill, to go at it hammer and tongs, to work like a nailer, to throw on the scrapheap, to have an axe to grind, to hit the nail on the head, to have a screw loose, to blow off steam, to keep his nose to the grindstone.* Cf. *a live wire; to step on it; a high flier,* etc. Characteristic idioms from the arts are: *to put the finishing touches to a thing, to change one's tune, to buy for a song, to act a part, to be in the limelight, to give the show away.* Mercantile proverbial phrases are more frequent than mercantile proverbs, e. g. *to strike a balance, to get more than one bargained for, to make the best of a bad bargain, to make capital of, to turn the scales, to talk shop, to call to account, to take into account, to pay him back in his own coin, to ring true, to give it the acid test* (the pawnbroker tests gold with acid). The number derived from schools and books is comparatively small: *to give chapter and verse, to turn over a new leaf, to take a leaf out of his book, to gloss over, to read a lecture to, to read between the lines, to put a period to.* Even the American Indians have given us *to smoke the pipe of peace, to bury the hatchet, to go on the warpath.*

Many such phrases are extremely obscure in their origins and offer unsolved problems. Of course the meaning and history of a phrase can only be determined on the basis of a careful and relatively large collection of instances. A thorough familiarity with the age of a saying, its degree of popularity, and the circles in which it is known are of invaluable assistance in discovering its meaning. Unfortunately the dictionaries and collections of proverbs at our disposal often fail or mislead us in just these respects. Proverbial phrases are very often passed over with slight attention by lexicographers.

It is instructive to examine briefly a number of proverbial phrases for which we have no adequate explanation. The Elizabethan *to lead apes in hell* was synonymous with being an old maid, and, although it was once a commonplace, we no longer understand the allusion.   The German synonyms *Giritzenmoos* and *Flederwische feilhalten* ('to offer dustbrushes for sale') are equally obscure. Other imperfectly understood English proverbial phrases are: *to be at sixes and sevens, to leave one in the lurch, to be in a brown study, to be up to snuff,* i. e. 'to be clever,' *to cast sheep's eyes on, to make no bones about a thing,* i. e. 'to treat it without formality,' *to have a rod in pickle, to fight like Kilkenny cats,* which may involve an old story with parallels in Icelandic saga, *to kick the bucket* and *to go West,* i. e. 'to die,' *to give him the sack* (in England: *bag*), i. e. 'to discharge from employment,' *to be duck soup for him,* which resembles its German equivalent *Das ist ihm ein gefundenes Fressen* in form and substance, *to be an Indian giver,* i. e. 'to demand the return of a gift,' *to paint the town red,* which, although not recorded before 1877, may have some connection with the ancient use of red as a festival color, *to take French leave* (the French idiom is *Filer à l'anglaise*). *To read him the Riot Act* refers to the actual reading aloud which precedes the dispersing of a mob in England.[1] The phrase *to call a spade a spade* may allude to a spayed dog, and possibly we can find support for this explanation in the synonymous Italian *to call a cat a cat* (chiamar gatta gatta).   On the other hand, the

1 See Act for Preventing Tumults and Riotous Assemblies, 1714.
1 George I, St. 2, ch. 5, §2, par. 2 (13 Statutes at Large, p. 143).

German *to show him what a rake is* (einem zeigen was eine Harke ist) suggests that "spade" means a garden implement. Chaucer has several obscure phrases for which no one has found an explanation: *Farwel felde-fare, to pipe in an ivy leafe, hazlewodss shaken*.

Often the explanations given for proverbial phrases are scarcely convincing or involve matters which after all we do not understand much better than the phrase itself. There may be an allusion to a forgotten game in *to hold a candle to*, i. e. 'to be compared with.' In the case of *to get a thing by hook or by crook* it is not quite clear what significance attaches to the fact that the earliest instances have ecclesiastical associations. Certainly that fact has been neglected by those who find in it an allusion to a manorial privilege granted certain dependants of using a hook to cut the green wood and a crook to break off the dry. Perhaps *to be driven* (var. *beaten*) *from pillar to post* refers to the treatment of Christ before the Crucifixion. The scene was presumably a familiar one from the representations of Biblical dramas. But an allusion from the end of the sixteenth century does not accord well with this explanation: "tossed from post to pillar like an espial or runagate" suggests rather an origin in a punishment like running the gauntlet. Much greater probability attaches to the explanation of *to make ducks and drakes of his money*, which finds in it an allusion to the term "ducks and drakes" for the circles made by a stone skimming across the water. Perhaps to mind your P's and Q's refers to the innkeeper's account of P[ints] and Q[uarts], although some have maintained that it is an idiom of the dancing school where attention was constantly being called to "pieds" and "queues." An explanation which is more probable than either of these finds the origin in the difficulty which the typesetter has in keeping P's and Q's from getting mixed. Obviously more knowledge of the circumstances under which a proverbial phrase is used (particularly in its early occurrences) helps greatly to make such matters clear. As it now is, in many instances *yo' pays yo' money and yo' takes yo' choice*.

Many unexplained phrases are internationally known and offer especially attractive opportunities for investigation. With the light thrown on the phrase from different angles it ought to be possible to discover its meaning easily. Yet the many long discussions of the phrase *to wear horns*, i. e. 'to be a cuckold,' have not made its origin clear; probably the trick of grafting spurs on a capon will explain it. One of the most interesting of such phrases is *wissen wo Barthel den Most holt* ('to be very sly and clever'; 'to know ways and means to attain one's end,' often with sexual implications; lit. 'to know where Barthel gets new wine'), for which several explanations have been offered. It may involve an allusion to St. Bartholomew's Day (August 24), which marks the beginning of autumn (although new wine is not made at that time), or to the marriage at Cana in Galilee which, according to tradition (but not *John* ii), was held in the house of Bartholomew. Probably the most generally accepted explanation bases itself on thieves' jargon and interprets "Barthel" as 'jimmy' (a thief's tool) and "Most" as 'money'; hence the phrase may have originally meant 'to know where one can get money by housebreaking.' If this explanation is correct, then the Dutch variant *weten wel waer Abraham de mostaerd haelt* ('to know well where Abraham gets mustard') is merely a corruption in popular speech. *To put a spoke in his wheel* is said to be a mistranslation of the Dutch *Er is eene spaak in het wiel gestoken.* The phrase *leben wie der liebe Gott in Frankreich* ('to live like the blessed Lord in France'), which is current both in Germany and in the Netherlands, has found no convincing explanation. Since it is at least as old as 1771, it cannot refer to the leisure given to God by the atheists of the French Revolution.

Ordinarily the distribution of phrases which are difficult to explain does not extend beyond the boundaries of a single language. In addition to the English examples of obscure phrases, I cite a few from the German: *einen Metzergang machen*, i. e. 'to make a journey in vain'; *im Schwabenalter stehen*, i. e. 'to be forty years old'; *auf keinen grünen Zweig kommen*, i. e. 'not to prosper.' From the fifteenth century on, and apparently more frequently in southern than in northern Germany, one summoned vexatious opponents to the valley of Josaphat (*ins Tal Josaphat laden*), but an explanation of the phrase is not forthcoming beyond the fact that the Last Judgment is meant. We may compare the English exclamation *Go to Jericho!* The phrase *von Pontius zu Pilatus schicken* evidently alludes to the treatment of Christ before the Crucifixion, but the exact way in which the phrase arose is not understood. Perhaps it alludes to scenes in the mediaeval Passion Play in which Christ goes from Herod to Pontius Pilate and from Pontius Pilate to Herod. The proverbial phrase *flöten gehen*, i. e. '[he can] whistle for it,' has been the occasion for much fruitless discussion.

Of course great interest attaches to proverbial phrases which concern themselves with the life of former days. Examples have already been given incidentally, but additional illustration is not out of place here. Perhaps *to take the cake* (or *That takes the cake*), a phrase which Aristophanes uses more than once, alludes to a cake as a prize for the man who stayed awake until sunrise in a drinking bout; we of today are more likely to find in it an echo of the custom of the "cake-walk." An older phrase of the same meaning is *to bear the bell*. The phrase *to throw dust in his eyes*, which is first found in classical writers, refers to a trick of gladiators. When Chaucer's Wife of Bath says "As by the whelp chasted is the leoun" and Iago, "Even so as one would beat his defenseless dog to affright an imperious lion," they use a Latin prover-

bial phrase based on the animal tamer's way of tam-
ing a lion by example. The English idiom *to curry
favor* refers to a famous horse, Fauvel, in a forgotten
French romance. *To pay on the nail* is an old French
legal phrase. German humanists who read Tacitus'
description of heathen German life with keen interest
are supposed to have invented *auf der Bärenhaut
liegen*, i. e. 'to be idle.' *Den armen Judas singen*, i. e.
'to sing the air of "Poor Judas,"' and then 'to suffer
great humiliation,' was an idiom current in the sixteenth century and used, appropriately enough, of
Faust just before his death. The queer German
phrase *einen Korb bekommen*, i. e. 'to get a basket, to
be refused in marriage, to fail in an examination,' is
now explained as an allusion to a mediaeval story of
Virgil. He was left suspended in a basket by a lady to
whom he was paying court. Other idioms meaning
'to refuse in marriage' are *to give him the mitten*, the
Spanish *dar una calabaza*, i. e. 'to give him a cala-
bash.' More or less obvious paraphrases like *to give
him his walking papers* or *ticket* (compare the Dutch
iemand zijn pasport geven) and the French *faire pro-
mener* are less interesting.

In proverbial phrases perhaps even more frequently
than in proverbs we have allusions to traditional
superstitions and the beliefs of former ages: *to be born
under a lucky star* refers to astrological notions; *to be
in the seventh heaven* involves the old cosmology; and
to shed crocodile tears is explained by the old belief

that crocodiles enticed unwary men into their power by imitating a weeping child. The proverbial phrase *Some one is walking over my grave*, which involves a widely known superstition, is used on feeling a sudden shiver. *Mit einem Helm geboren sein* ('to be born with a caul') alludes to the belief that such children are unusually lucky; we have an analogous phrase in English: *to be born with a silver spoon in his mouth*. A legal allusion persists in *to come under the hammer*, which refers to the auctioneer's hammer.

The explanation of historical allusions in proverbial phrases often leaves much room for doubt, although it seems likely that historical details are better preserved in phrases than in proverbs. Perhaps the German *to burn his ships behind him* (Seine Schiffe hinter sich brennen) refers to Cortez in Mexico in 1519, but the existence of parallel incidents extending so far back as 310 B.C. makes the identification uncertain in the extreme. The English *to burn his bridges behind him* also stands in some unexplained relation to the German idiom. The appropriation of the lands of St. Peter at Westminster to pay for the repair of St. Paul's in the reign of Edward VI can hardly account for the phrase *to rob Peter to pay Paul*. In French and German, the allusion would be unintelligible, and furthermore the early variant form, French and English, *to rob St. Peter to clothe St. Paul*, must be considered in any explanation of origins.

As is already abundantly apparent, proverbial

phrases come into being in the same ways as proverbs.
A phrase with limited application acquires by metaphorical use a meaning in new fields: *to kill two birds
with one stone* acquires in addition to its literal meaning the connotation of accomplishing two ends with
the same instrument. Most proverbial phrases have
arisen in this way. Proverbial phrases are also derived from narratives, e. g. *to bell the cat*, i. e. 'to
undertake a dangerous task.' Often these narratives
have a long and checkered history. In Arabic the
story behind the phrases *to pull the chestnuts out of
the fire* and *to be a cat's paw* has a crab instead of
chestnuts, and this form found its way into Italian in
the *Fables of Bidpai* (the *Pañcatantra*). Other variants in Italian and in Dutch read "snake" instead of
"crab" or "chestnuts." The substitution of the cat
seems to have occurred in France. Perhaps, as has
been conjectured, "cat" is a misunderstanding of the
Latin *catellus* 'whelp,' for a dog is found in several
texts.

Although probably less frequent, the changes which
occur in proverbial phrases during their life in oral
tradition are of the same general character as the
changes in proverbs. Ordinarily proverbial phrases
do not accumulate expansions by parallelism and
contrast with the same readiness as do proverbs, but
such an extension as *to have a crow to pluck with you
and a poke to put the feathers in* is analogous to the
whimsical enlargement of proverbs. Of course sub-

stitutions of similar and contrasting objects after the
manner of associative thought take place readily.

Analogous to proverbs which are used only in certain definite connections are proverbial phrases with
a single connotation. An important class of such
phrases is found in paraphrases for drunkenness, e. g.
*to be jingled, soused, half seas over, all teed up, lit,
pickled, pie-eyed, crocked, corned* (referring to corn
whiskey), *three sheets in the wind, over the bay, to pass
out.*[1] It is possibly true that synonyms for drunkenness are more abundant in German than in English
or French, but the fact, if it is one, is an uncertain
basis for conclusions regarding the temperance of a
people.

WELLERISMS [2]

A very curious proverbial type has, so far as I am
aware, no English name, although it is well repre-

[1] Proverbial phrases signifying "drunken" have been collected in several
places: Bohn, *A Hand-book of Proverbs*, 1855, p. 63; Prenner, *American
Speech*, IV (1929), 102–103; H. Schudt, "Er ist betrunken," *Hessische
Blätter für Volkskunde*, XXVII (1928), 76–89; Friedli, *Bärndütsch*, V
(1922), 455–494; Unfeld, *Zeitschrift für Deutsche Mundarten*, VII (1906),
177–182; K. Rother, *Die Schlesischen Sprichwörter und Redensarten*
(Breslau, 1928), pp. 103–108; H. Schrader, *Das Trinken in mehr als
500 Gleichnissen und Redensarten* (Berlin, 1896); Woeste, "Nieder-
deutsche Ausdrücke für 'trunken sein,'" *Die Deutschen Mundarten*,
V (1858), 67–74; Harrebomée, *Bacchus in Spreekwoordentaal* (Gorinchem, 1874); J. Cornelissen, "De dronkenschap in de volkstaal,"
Ons Volksleven, IX (1897), 48–49.

[2] Collections devoted solely to Wellerisms are not numerous and are
limited to German and Swedish: Hoefer, *Wie das Volk Spricht: 524
Sprichwörtliche Redensarten* (Stuttgart, 1855; the recent undated
eighth edition contains more than 2, 100 Wellerisms); G. H[olmström],

sented in English and American oral tradition.[1] Yet
curiously enough when Moritz Haupt, professor of
classical languages and literatures at Berlin, lectured
on a line in Theocritus in which one of these proverbs
occurs, he said "A certain Samuel Weller of Dickens
uses many English [proverbs of this sort]" (Anglicis
plurimis utitur vel unus ille Dickensii Samuel Wel-
lerus).[2] With such authority to support us we may call
these proverbs Wellerisms. To be sure, the observation that they are characteristic of Sam Weller is by

Sa Han och Sa Hon (Stockholm, 1876, 2nd ed., 1880, 3rd ed., 1890);
Schultz, Sex Hundra Ordstäv (Stockholm, ca. 1860); Woeste, Die Deut-
schen Mundarten, III (1856), 253–264, V (1858), 57–66; H. Herzog,
Beispielssprichwörter(Aarau, 1882). Collections of ordinary proverbs
often give Wellerisms a place apart, e. g. Norway: R. T. Christiansen,
Gamle Visdomsord (Oslo, 1928), pp. 83–87; Denmark: E. T. Kristensen,
Danske Ordsprog (Copenhagen, 1890), pp. 633–650; England: Lean,
Collectanea, II, 741–752. Particular interest attaches to collections
from certain regions in Germany where Wellerisms are less frequent
than in northern Germany; see, e. g. Berthold, Hessische Blätter für
Volkskunde, XXIII (1924), 113–115; A. Becker, Pfälzer Volkskunde
(Bonn, 1925), p. 169.
  Studies devoted to Wellerisms are, as follows. General: Seiler, Lehn-
sprichwort, VIII, 1ff.; Classical: M. Haupt, Opuscula (Leipzig, 1876),
II, 395–406; Low German and Danish: P. Bartels, as cited by Seiler,
Zeitschrift für Deutsche Philologie, XLVIII (1920), 87, n. 1; Swedish:
Cederschiöld, Om Ordstäv och Andra Ämnen (Lund, 1923), pp. 5–33;
Kalén, "Några Utbyggda Ordstäv från Halland," Folkminnen och
Folktankar, XII, part 2 (1925), 27–38. Hoefer's introductory essay to
Wie das Volk Spricht is not in the first, anonymous edition (pace
Seiler) and is alluded to as an omission from the eighth edition; the
long introduction by Max Bruns in the recent undated edition under
the title Der Volksmund is not particularly helpful.
1 German has also struggled with the problem of naming this type of
  proverb and has called it variously "Beispielssprichwort," "apolo-
  gisches Sprichwort," and "Sagwort."
2 Opuscula (Leipzig, 1876), II, 405.

no means original with Haupt. The examples in the *Pickwick Papers* had already been brought together in 1867, and presumably the proverbs collected under the title "Samwelleriana" in a Dutch periodical, *Het Leeskabinet*, of 1863, belong to the same class.[1] But long before Dickens the existence of the type in England is attested by a story about Queen Elizabeth and the first collection of English proverbs. Tradition relates that John Heywood presented his collection to her. She asked whether every English proverb was included and he assured her that he knew of no omission. She in turn offered to wager that she could name a proverb he had overlooked. The proverb which she had in mind, namely, *Bate me an ace, quoth Bolton*, was actually missing. Heywood might have defended himself by saying that it belonged to a very special class of proverbs which he would have found it difficult or even impossible to use in his verses, although he does find room for "*Backare*," *quoth Mortimer to his sow*. Essential characteristics are the phrase "quoth Bolton" and the humorous turn, which in this particular instance escapes us. The meaning and connotation of Queen Elizabeth's proverb are now entirely lost, notwithstanding its frequent occurrence in writings of that age. Heywood's Wellerism is, moreover, not the earliest example in

1 Maass, "39 Odd Similes aus dem Pickwick Papers von Charles Dickens," *Archiv für das Studium der Neueren Sprachen*, XLI (1867), 207–215; Harrebomée, *Spreekwoordenboek der Nederlandsche Taal* (Utrecht, 1858–70), III, cccxv.

English. Nearly two centuries before, Chaucer wrote
in *Troilus and Criseyde*:

> Lat this proverbe a lore unto you be:
> "To late y-war!" quod Beaute, whan it paste.
>
> ii, 397–398.

In the *Canterbury Tales* he uses "'Soth play, quad
play,' as the Flemyng saith."

Wellerisms are far older than these English quotations, for examples from Latin and Greek literature can be pointed out. Indeed Seiler even goes so
far as to maintain that the modern traditional forms
have descended to us from classical antiquity. Latin
and Greek examples are not very numerous, but their
resemblance to the type is unmistakable. A few illustrations are "*All the women we need are inside,*" said
the bridegroom and closed the door on the bride (Theocritus, xv, 77); "*The water will tell you,*" said the guide
when the travelers asked him how deep the river was
(Plato, *Theaet.*, 200 E); "*Farewell, dear light,*" said
*the lustful old woman as she undressed and put out the
light* (Zenobius, vi, 42);[1] "*That is too much business,*"
said the broker; he had seen six policemen (Laberius,
frag. 63, in Aulus Gellius, xvi, 7, 12). Perhaps Livy

---

[1] The point of the witticism lies in the fact that she used the conventional
dying words of a tragic figure. We may compare the conventional farewell in ballads of executions, e. g.

> Got gesegne dich, Sunn! Got gesegne dich, Mon!
> Got gesegne dich, schönes Lieb, wa ich dich hon!
> Ich muss mich von dir scheiden.

See O. Böckel, *Handbuch des Deutschen Volkslieds* (1908), p. 132.

(xxiii, 47) alludes to a proverb of this sort in his account of the meeting of Taurea and Claudius: 'when Taurea finds that Claudius takes him at his word, he pretends that his proposal to fight on the road was merely a joke, saying, "By your leave, I will not throw my horse into a ditch" (Minime, sis, inquit, cantherinum in fossam).' These words, Livy tells us, became a proverb. Less than a score of classical examples are known. It is not clear whether classical rhetoricians recognized the form. Possibly Quintilian was referring to it when he said: "παροιμίας that sort which is briefer like a fable and is understood allegorically: '*It is not our burden*,' *said the ox*, [*looking*] *at the saddle*" (παροιμίας genus illud, quod est velut fabella brevior et per allegoriam accipitur: "non nostrum," inquit, "onus," bos clitellas, v, 11, 21). The use of a Greek term suggests that the concept was not familiar to him and possessed no Latin name.

The historical significance of these classical Wellerisms, and indeed the whole history of the form, is obscure. Seiler asserts categorically that the form is classical in origin, notwithstanding its apparently native vigor and originality in Germany and the adjoining Germanic countries. Cogent proof of classical descent is not forthcoming, unless it lie in the almost complete neglect of the form in the Middle Ages and its reappearance in the sixteenth century. The four oldest mediaeval examples, which are found in the monastic *Fecunda Ratis* of Egbert of Liège, show some affinity to classical story. But direct descent from the few classical Wellerisms cannot be made out. Between this time — the end of the eleventh century — and the rise of German Humanism in the sixteenth century instances are extremely rare. Seiler notes two, which are distinctly mediaeval and monastic rather than popular, and I may add *"Something is better than nothing,"* said the wolf when he swallowed the louse ("Plus valet il quam nil," pulicem gluciens lupus inquit) and others.[1] Perhaps this historical evidence supports Seiler's conjecture.

Yet we need not see a relation of cause and effect in the appearance of Wellerisms after the rise of Humanism in Germany. Here the *argumentum ex silentio* can, however, have little value. For at least two reasons Wellerisms found no place in the earliest German collections; in the first place, these collections are by south German authors who had little opportunity to know Wellerisms; and in the second

---

1 Examples of mediaeval Latin Wellerisms are much more frequent than Seiler's discussion would imply. The following instances have come to my attention: Müllenhoff and Scherer, *Denkmäler*[2], I, 45, No. 84 (In discendo lupus nimis affirmans ait "agnus"); 48, No. 161 ("Phi," sonuit fuscum ridens ardaria furnum); J. Werner, *Lateinische Sprichwörter und Sinnsprüche des Mittelalters* (Heidelberg, 1912), p. 9, No. C 42 (Clamat ocellus: "amat!" "dolet hic" manus anxia clamat); p. 25, No. D 189; p. 57, No. N 154; p. 96, No. S 211; J. Klapper, *Die Sprichwörter der Freidankpredigten* (Wort und Brauch, XVI), 1927, Nos. 61, 87, 151, 174, 329. The Wellerism which Goethe uses, *"Es ist schlecht Wasser,"* sagte der Reiher und konnte nicht schwimmen ("'Bad water," said the heron and couldn't swim'), was known in the Middle Ages; see Seiler, *Zeitschrift für den deutschen Unterricht*, XXXIII (1919), 383–386; Müllenhoff and Scherer, *Denkmäler*[2], I, 59, No. 13 and the note, II, 138.

place, the aims of these collections conflicted with the characteristic temper and tone of Wellerisms. The peculiar qualities which characterize the form, its often obscene humor and its lack of a moral or didactic turn, render it unsuitable for school use. Consequently there was no place for it in the early collections with primarily pedagogical or didactic aims. According to Seiler,[1] Luther believed the Devil was hostile to proverbs and seduced people by turning them into an evil form, the Wellerism. It is clear from Luther's marginal notes to his collection of proverbs that he regarded Wellerisms as malicious perversions, but there is no convincing evidence that Luther regarded Wellerisms as the work of the Devil.

The obvious conflict with morality causes the exclusion of Wellerisms from most later German collections of the sixteenth and seventeenth centuries. Their relative abundance in Neander's compilation of 1590 leads Seiler to believe that many Wellerisms were invented in the sixteenth century; but this is the *argumentum ex silentio.* Unfortunately the hundred instances from sixteenth-century literature which J. Franck said he could readily quote are lost along with the 250,000 sheets of collectanea.[2] Macaronic Weller-

1 *Lehnsprichwort,* VIII, 13.
2 See F. Latendorf, *L. v. Passavant gegen Agricola's Sprichwörter* (Berlin, 1873), p. 28. The collectanea of Franck were, from all reports, the most extensive ever made, but all trace of them has been lost; see Seiler, *Deutsche Sprichwörterkunde,* p. 147. Latendorf (*Michel Neanders Deutsche Sprichwörter* [Schwerin, 1864]) gives some fifty Wellerisms from the sixteenth century.

isms like *"Barbati praecedant," sagte Magister Fuchs, stiess einen Bock die Treppe hinunter* ('"Let gray-beards go first," said Master Fox [and] pushed a goat down the steps'); *"Virtus in medio," sagte der Teufel, sass zwischen zwei alten Huren* ('"Virtue in the middle," said the Devil [and] sat between two old harlots'), which Seiler quotes from Neander, are cited to show the humanistic associations of the form. But these macaronic witticisms seem to be clever inventions rather than the germ from which the type developed. We can certainly conclude that humanists were well disposed toward the Wellerism, but the evidence does not permit us to declare that they were responsible for it. Inasmuch as Neander came from Silesia, a region in which the folk still show a marked predilection for Wellerisms, it is difficult to know whether his evident liking for the form is better explained by his humanistic training or by his native bent. The latter seems much more probable.

In sum, the history of the Wellerism as a type is obscure and difficult to trace. We have thus far been concerned only with classical, mediaeval, and German instances. Examples from other countries and ages are little known and studied. Before going farther, it will be wise to examine the distribution of the type.

The distribution of Wellerisms is very curious. We have more information about the state of affairs in Germany than elsewhere. A liking for Wellerisms distinguishes northern Germany as far south as Hesse. Hoefer's *Wie das Volk spricht*, which is the most important collection, contains nearly 2,100 numbers, and of these more than half are Low German. The Wellerism is popular along the Rhine and in the later-colonized areas in the East, notably Silesia. As we have seen, this fact may explain Neander's liking for the form; he was born at Sorau, in Lusatia. Sebastian Frank's large collection and the others of the sixteenth century with which Seiler makes comparisons are without exception middle and south German. The first north German collections are didactic and have no room for Wellerisms. The exact southern boundary is not known, nor is it possible of determination like the boundary of a linguistic detail. Instances are known from Hesse, Baden, and even from Bavaria and Switzerland. Certainly the manner in which they are mentioned implies that the form is rare in those regions. A careful study of local proverb collections might give us more information, although the frequency with which Wellerisms are excluded must be reckoned with. A close examination of the forms reported from southern Germany might be instructive: we might find them awkward and unskilfully made. A study of the variants of some widely known Wellerisms might reveal the ways in which they spread.

In northern Germany and Scandinavia the Wellerism is very popular. We know very little about its currency in other regions. The few mediaeval instances owe their dissemination to Latin and have for the most part become extinct. The toad and harrow supply the materials for perhaps the only mediaeval Latin Wellerism which still has any importance in tradition. In English it circulates as "*Many masters,*" *quoth the toad to the harrow when every tine turned her over.* This saying goes back as far as the eleventh-century *Fecunda Ratis.* The long history of "Nos poma natamus," which is perhaps known to English readers in the mistranslation "*We apples are swimming,*" *said the horse-chestnut and swam down the stream with the apples* or in the utterly unintelligible "*How we apples swim,*" is international and begins in the sixteenth century. Martin Luther did not disdain to use it against an opponent; and before him it finds an appropriate place in the satiric handbooks of inverted etiquette: Dedekind's *Grobianus* (1549) and the translation by Kaspar Scheit (1551).

Generally speaking, parallels to Wellerisms from several countries are much rarer than parallels to ordinary proverbs. There are, to be sure, Swedish and Dutch variants and even a Frisian one of 1691 for the English "*Many a thing is made for a penny,*" *as the old wife said when she saw the black man.* Ordinarily we can speak of the international dissemination of Wellerisms only with reservations and with reference to particular sayings.

English Wellerisms are collected by Lean.[1] John
Galsworthy uses one in the *Forsyte Saga*, III, i, ch.
xii: "'Fini,' as the French girl said when she jumped
on her bed after saying her prayers," and Thomas
Hardy has others in his Wessex novels. In addition
to those cited already, we may mention "*Nay, stay,*"
quoth Stringer, when his neck was in the halter;
"*Ahem!*" *as Dick Smith said, when he swallowed the
dishcloth*; "*I'll tent* (probe?) *thee,*" *quoth Wood*; "*If I
can't rule my daughter, I'll rule my good*"; "*Go away
here, go away there,*" *quoth Madge Whitworth, when she
rode the mare in the tedder*; "*I'll make one,*" *quoth
Kirkham, when he danced in his clogs.* In the *Shortest
Way with the Dissenters* Defoe used one which has a
long history: "*Pray, good folk, let us not step on each
other,*" *said the cock* [*to the horse*]. Although examples
in modern British and American oral tradition have
not been recorded in any abundance, the type is not
entirely unknown, e. g. "*Everyone to his taste,*" *said
the farmer and kissed the cow*; "*Neat but not gaudy,*"
said the monkey (var. *Devil*) *when he painted his tail
blue*; "*All's well that ends well,*" *said the peacock when
he looked at his tail.*

So far as I can learn, French Wellerisms have never
been collected. Probably the rarity of the form in
French accounts for this lack of interest. In a notice

of one of Seiler's books on proverbs, Arnold van Gennep declares that proverbs of this sort are found in French tradition, but he cites only one example: *"Oh! Oh!" said the Portuguese* ("Oh! Oh!" dit le portugais). Perhaps Rabelais was using a Wellerism when he wrote *"Appetite comes from eating," said Angest on Mans, "and thirst from drinking"* ("L'appetit vient en mangeant," dit Angest on Mans, "et la soif en buvant," *Gargantua*, I, ch. v). In Balzac's *Les Paysans* we find the following example: *"You mustn't spit on the harvest," as Papa Noah said* ("Faut pas cracher zur la vendange!" a dit le papa Noé, ch. iv). Since we have a collection of Spanish proverbial and traditional phrases containing proper names (L. Montoto y Rautenstrauch, *Personajes, personas y personillas que corren por las tierras de ambas Castillas* [Seville, 1911–13]) in which Wellerisms should be recorded if they exist, we may conclude that they are practically unknown. Italian examples are difficult to find, e. g. *"Saran quest' anno di molte pere," diceva l'orso, perchè n'harebbe volute* ('"There will be many pears this year," said the bear because that was his wish'); *"Adagio," disse il Fibbia* ('"Slow," said Fibbia'). A few others, which do not seem to be very characteristic examples, have been mentioned in the remarks on the connections of fables and proverbs.

Scandinavian tradition revels in the Wellerism. Many of the important collections of Danish, Ice-

landic, Norwegian, and Swedish proverbs devote a
special section to it. The early vernacular examples
are interesting and historically important, e. g. *"Such
things often happen at sea,"* said the seal, [when] it was
shot in the eye (Opt verðr slíkt á sæ, kvað selr, var
skotinn í auga), which occurs in the *Fornmannasögur*
of the late twelfth century.¹ At the end of the twelfth
century King Magnus Barfot sent one of his followers
to southern Bohuslän to induce the people to submit
peacefully to his authority. After listening to the
emissary's speech to the assembly, someone in the
audience answered, *"The snow will come soon, lads,"*
said the Finns [and] had skis for sale ("Snart kommer
snön, svenner," sa finnarna, hade skidor till salu).
And on the same occasion another man said, *"No
roller is needed,"* said the raven [and] pulled a mussel-
shell on the ice ("Behövs ingen rulle," sa räven, drog
musselskalet på isen). An allusion to a house raising
or some similar custom in which neighbors join to help
one another is found in a Wellerism in a fifteenth
century Swedish collection: *"The assistance would be
good, if they only didn't eat so much,"* said the old
woman (Hjälpen vore nog god, ginge bara inte maten
åt," sa käringen).²

It has not been noticed that the Celts employ the
Wellerism with evident ease and freedom, as the fol-

---

1 Finnur Jónsson ("Oldislandske Ordsprog og Talemåder," *Arkiv för
Nordisk Filologi*, XXX [1914], 71, No. 44; 105, No. 228) gives two later
Icelandic examples.
2 The language is slightly modernized.

lowing Gaelic examples show: "*If this be human, it's light*," as the waterhorse said; "*I'm not a soldier and don't wish to be*," as the fox said to the wolf; "*Mair haste, the less speed*," quo' the wee tailor to the lang thread; "*Blow for blow*," as Conan said to the Devil. A few Lettish examples are quoted by Gustav Meyer in commenting on the preference which Greek proverbs show for the narrative form, e. g. "*Now we have rowed well*," said the flea, when the fisher drew the boat on land.[1] To this we have an English parallel in "*What a dust I have raised*," quoth the fly upon the coach, which Bacon (Essay 54) credits to Æsop: "It was prettily derided by Æsope; *The Fly sate upon the Axle-tree of the Chariot wheele, and said, What a dust as I raise?*"[2]

The Wellerism describes a scene with such vividness that it is clearly brought home to us, although we may not be able to catch the full implications, as in the Elizabethan "*Backare*," quoth Mortimer to his sow. Its relation to historical fact is often close. Cederschiöld is able to trace a number of Swedish instances back to their origins: "*Inte ett dugg*," sa Settervall refers, for example, to an incident in the Swedish financial crisis of 1857. Settervall examined

---

1 "Zu den Mittelgriechischen Sprichwörtern," *Byzantinische Zeitschrift*, III (1894), 400. Meyer, who is following Crusius ("Märchenreminiszenzen im Antiken Sprichwort," *Verhandlungen der 40. Versammlung Deutscher Philologen zu Görlitz* [1889], p. 40), seems to confuse the Greek narrative proverb with the Wellerism; see also p. 159 above.
2 The reference to Æsop is found in Romulus, ii, 17 (ed. Oesterley, p. 60).

the accounts in the presence of his partner, Dugge. Dugge asked anxiously, "Can you find anything left?" "Not a drop" (Inte ett dugg), said Settervall. In *Hemsöborna,* a novel of peasant life on the small islands along the Swedish coast, Strindberg gives a graphic description of the origin of a Wellerism: neither of the farm-hands, Carlsson and Rundqvist, liked to work, but in order to gain favor they did many small tasks about the house. Finally Carlsson seemed to have won the day by painting the fireplace white. Not to be outdone, the duller Rundqvist painted an outhouse a brilliant red. The household saw the humorous side of it all and someone coined the phrase: "One should begin at the right end," said Rundqvist, and painted the outhouse first ("Man ska börja i rätta ändan," sa Rundqvist, strök avträdet först, *Hemsöborna,* ch. iii). We need not try to show that this is actually a traditional Wellerism. It suffices that the manner of invention suggests the ways in whichth e traditional forms arise. A Dutch Welerlism, "*Give me time,*" *said Koekkbakker* ("Geeft tijd," zei Koekkbakker), which is more than two centuries old, can also be traced to a definite incident in business. When his creditors suspected his honesty, Koekbakker, a resident of Middelburg (a town near the mouth of the Schelde), reassured them by saying, "Give me time," and fled with all his money the next night. We need not fear greatly to trust the story or one of the stories told to explain "*The case is altered,*"

quoth Plowden. I tell the shorter one: Edmund Plowden, an eminent barrister in Queen Elizabeth's time,
answered a neighbor that there was very good remedy
in law for hogs that trespassed. But when the neighbor went on to say that the hogs were Plowden's own,
"Nay, then, neighbor," quoth Plowden, "the case is
altered." Probably we cannot verify the truth of this
narrative, but we need not hesitate to believe that the
saying sprang from this incident or a similar one.
"Bate me an ace," quoth Bolton becomes more intelligible when we know that a John Bolton was "one of
Henry VIII's diverting rascals."

Kalén declares that he has been able to trace
practically every Wellerism in oral tradition in the
Swedish province of Halland back to a definite personal allusion when the Wellerism gives a clue in a
proper name. Notwithstanding this close relation to
historical events, it does not appear that many Wellerisms have arisen as condensations of fables and
apologues. *"I punish my wife with good words," said
the peasant and threw the Bible at her head* (German
and Danish) is probably a reminiscence of an old
story which has attained international currency as a
Wellerism. The same is true of *"That's strong tobacco," said the Devil, when the hunter shot off his rifle
in the Devil's mouth.* Seiler is inclined to regard the
narrative element as often being present, but it is
very slight in some of his examples. Tuinman, a very
sensible Dutch commentator on proverbs in the first

quarter of the eighteenth century, regarded Wellerisms as closely related to Æsopic fables.¹ Such explanations apply to a very small number of Wellerisms. An interesting illustration is "*It's a day too
late*," *said the widow, when a servant-man proposed to
her at the funeral dinner; she had engaged herself to the
man who had made the coffin* ("De' er ein Dag for-
seint," sa Enkjan, daa Drengen friade till henne i
Gravölet — ho hadde lovat han, som gjorde Likki-
stan). This is an allusion to the world-old story of the
Ephesian widow which has been told from China to
Iceland.²

Probably the life of the ordinary Wellerism is very
short. An incident gives rise to a witty remark which
perpetuates itself for a space of time, but when the
circumstances have been forgotten or the names and
persons of those concerned have ceased to be suggestive, the saying passes out of existence. Only a few
Wellerisms enjoy a wide currency, and these are often
based on some internationally intelligible allusion or
a witticism so obvious that it needs no commentary.
The great majority of Wellerisms probably never
gain currency beyond very narrow confines.

We may examine the Wellerism as regards subject

---

1 See Seiler, *Sprichwörterkunde*, p. 27; *Lehnsprichwort*, VIII, 3–4; Tuinman, *De Oorsprong en Uitlegging van Dagelyks Gebruikte Nederduitsche
Spreekwoorden*, I, 176. An illustration of Seiler's method will be found
in *Zeitschrift für Deutsche Philologie*, XLVIII (1919–20), 87, No. 1.

2 For references to this story see Killis Campbell, *The Seven Sages of
Rome* (Boston, 1907), pp. ci–cviii; Chauvin, *Bibliographie des Ouvrages
Arabes* (Liège), VIII (1904), 210; IX (1905), 92.

and form. Essential to it is the incongruity of combining a sober assertion with an utterly inappropriate scene. This incongruity often leads to obscenity and sardonic humor. Typical examples of humor are *"These are fine cuffs,"* said the thief of his handcuffs ("De va fina manchetter," sa tjuven om handklovarna); *"This week is beginning splendidly,"* said one who was to be hanged on Monday ("Den här veckan börjar trevligt," sa han, som skulle hängas på måndagen). Seiler's detailed analysis of the kinds of incongruities employed in Wellerisms does not, it seems to me, reveal significant facts, and it does not encourage one to pursue the subject further.[1]

The freedom and scant respect which Wellerisms display toward women, particularly old women, show that the form is a masculine invention in which women have had little share. Such sayings as *"Give her her will or she will burst,"* quoth the good man, when his wife was dinging him are characteristic. Perhaps this attitude toward women reflects the temper of an earlier age. We see something of the same sort in the treatment of the priest: *"Virtue in the middle,"* said the Devil and seated himself between two priests; *"Bad company,"* said the thief, as he went to the gallows between the hangman and the monk (Dutch). Such attitudes may merely represent the manners and thoughts of the peasant of any age. In the last two

1 Seiler, *Lehnsprichwort*, VIII, ch. vii, "Inhaltliche Gruppierung des Sagworts," 24–53.

examples it is interesting to observe that the same model has been used before in other connections; but it is not easy to find Wellerisms fashioned after already existing forms.

Stylistic consideration of Wellerisms may be based on form as well as content. Kalén's interesting observations on Wellerisms from the province of Halland show what can be accomplished in this direction, although it is not clear how far his conclusions are generally applicable.[1] He points out that there are two types of Wellerisms, those in which the allusion requires an indication of the scene, the speaker, or the object to which reference is made, and those in which no additional details are given. An English example of the first kind is *"Neat but not gaudy," said the monkey, as he painted his tail blue,* and of the second kind, *"The case is altered," quoth Plowden.* His article gives an illuminating analysis of the first and more abundant kind. All Wellerisms in which a proper name appears are, he finds, of comparatively recent origin. They have not spread very far and are ordinarily capable of immediate explanation. An older stratum is distinguished by naming the speaker with a pronoun or a title based on sex, age, or a trade. Probably Wellerisms in which an animal speaks are to be assigned to this older stratum. Of course these older Wellerisms can no longer be explained from al-

1 "Några utbyggda ordstäv," *Folkminnen och Folktankar,* XII (1925), No. 2, 27–38.

lusions to definite individuals or incidents and they
include those sayings which have won wider dissemination. On examining the three subdivisions in which
the allusion is explained by a temporal clause, a relative clause, or a prepositional phrase, Kalén finds that
very curious distinctions can be made. Wellerisms
involving a temporal clause, e. g. *"Much noise and
little wool," said the Devil when he sheared a pig*, are
largely used of women, although men and boys are
occasionally mentioned. Here the speaker is often
designated by age, sex, or trade. In sayings with a
relative clause, e. g. *"The week is beginning well," said
one who was to be hanged on Monday*, we rarely find
any designation of the speaker other than a proper
name or a pronoun, and women are mentioned very
infrequently. Sayings which employ a prepositional
phrase, e. g. *"These are fine cuffs," said the thief of his
handcuffs*, ordinarily refer to a thing and much more
rarely to a person; when the speaker's name is replaced by a pronoun or some other vague designation,
they concern themselves almost exclusively with
things. How these striking differences came about
remains to be discovered. Perhaps similar differences
can be found in Wellerisms from other regions.
Kalén's classification cannot be directly applied to
English and German Wellerisms; but a search for
analogous principles is likely to be fruitful.

Wellerisms which give no accompanying details are
not examined by Kalén. Typical examples are *"God*

help the fool," quoth Pedley; *"Backare,"* quoth Mortimer to his sow; *" Ei wer möchte das nicht,"* sagte der Abt
von Posen. These may represent the first stage in the
growth of a Wellerism. So long as the allusion is immediately intelligible, — in other words, so long as
Pedley is remembered as the court fool, — no ex-
planatory clause or phrase is needed. Just so soon as
the point of the witticism is no longer obvious, the
time, the speaker, or the thing spoken of must be
indicated.

We may perhaps recognize a special group of Wellerisms in those which use already existing proverbs,
e. g. *"Every little helps,"* said Mr. Little and took the
six little Littles out to help him saw a pile of wood;
"Like will to like," quoth the Devil to the collier; *"To
err is human,"* said the housewife and shook ground
pepper in the coffee; *"Much noise and little wool,"* said
the Devil and sheared a pig (*"Viel Geschrei und wenig
Wolle,"* sagte der Teufel und schor ein Schwein).
Obviously the proverb is older than the Wellerism,
for part of the humor arises from the presence of a
sober proverb in such surroundings.

Proverbial Comparisons [1]

Comparisons which we may call proverbial are
many and varied. In connection with them, just as
with proverbs, questions regarding origin, history,

1 Special collections are not numerous: see Wilstack, *A Dictionary of
Similes* (London, 1917); Lean, *Collectanea*, II, 753–895; Woeste, *Die
deutschen Mundarten*, V (1858), 57–66; Zingerle, *Die Deutschen Sprich-*

and form arise, but it is often difficult to collect
enough examples of a particular comparison to study
these questions effectively. Apparently the proverbial comparison offers fewer opportunities for study
than the proverb, although it seems probable that
something new can be learned by examining variations in taste from age to age. We see that the synonyms for "cold" or "white" differ at different
periods, but the variations have not been collected
and studied.

Ordinarily literal proverbial comparisons which
single out some obvious and familiar quality offer
little of interest, e. g. *as old as Methuselah*; *as quiet as
a mouse*; *as free as air*; *as dry as a bone*; *as hard as a
rock*; *as fat as a pig*; *as heavy as lead*; *as clear as crystal*.
Some literal comparisons are amusing in their whimsicality: *cold enough to freeze the tail off a brass monkey*;
as little chance as a snowball in Hell, or with still further expansion, *as little chance as a celluloid cat chasing
an asbestos dog in Hell*. Occasionally we find a proverbial comparison which has been made on the model
of another one, e. g. *as clear as mud*. Other proverbial comparisons find a similarity between an ethical
quality and an object: *as crooked* ('dishonest') *as a*

wörter im Mittelalter (Vienna, 1864); F. Rodríguez Marín, *Mil trescien-
tas comparaciones populares andaluzas* (Seville, 1899). Studies of
imagery in individual authors, e. g. Klaeber, *Das Bild bei Chaucer*
(Berlin, 1893), often include proverbial comparisons. See also Gabriel
Meurier, *La Perle des Similitudes* (Malines, 1583), which contains
866 comparisons with moral applications (cited from Bonser, *Proverb
Literature* [London, 1930], p. 127, No. 1061).

pretzel; *as good* ('virtuous') *as gold*; *as green* ('inexperienced') *as grass.*

Some proverbial comparisons offer interesting problems in interpretation: *as cold as sin* (euphemism for Hell?); *as dead as a door nail*; *as deaf as an adder* (implies a mediaeval superstition); *as cool as a cucumber*; *as ignorant as Thompson's colt.* For half a century inquirers in *Notes and Queries* have called for an explanation of *as thrang* ('hurried') *as Throp's wife*, but none has been forthcoming. Although I cannot give an explanation, this clue may lead to one. In the "Flyting of Dunbar and Kennedy" certain persons are named as fit relatives for Kennedy:

> Thy trew kynnismen, Antenor et Eneas,
> Throp thy nere nece, and austern Olibrius.[1]

No one has yet identified Throp. Since the Scotch "nece" may refer to a man, Throp may have had a wife about whom a story was told. *As crazy as Dick's hatband*, which is found in the variant form *As crazy as Dick's hatband which went round nine times and then wodn't tee*, is usually explained as an allusion to Richard Cromwell, Lord Protector of England; but the explanation is far from convincing. *As drunk as a lord* seems still to reflect the manners of old England. We cannot be sure what comparisons are worth the labor of seeking an interpretation: what shall we say of *as busy as a cranberry merchant*; *as*

[1] See Taylor, "Notes on the Wandering Jew," *Modern Language Notes,* XXXIII (1918), 394 ff.

thick ('intimate') *as hops* (perhaps because hops grow thickly); *as poor as Job's turkey* (var. *turkey hen*)?

Some proverbial comparisons have a long history and are widely used in poetry: *as red as blood*; *as white as snow*; *as green as grass*. Comparisons which involve colors can be readily traced through centuries of use.[1] Some variations in taste and meaning appear: *as green as grass* acquires in recent times the added meaning of "ignorant, inexperienced"; *as white as chalk* was once merely a comparison for "white," even for "shining white," while now it is ordinarily used of a dull white without gloss: "His face was as white as chalk." The comparison of green with the clover, which was long a commonplace of mediaeval poetry and later popular verse, is now little used, and *as white as a swan* or *as white as ermine* have perhaps a more poetic or artificial sound today than they once had. *As white as silver* is hardly known today, and *as white as a sheet* applies only to an unnatural pallor. The colloquial comparison *as brown as a berry* is as old as the twelfth century, and although some berries are brown, its appropriateness seems rather doubtful.

1 See I. V. Zingerle, "Farbenvergleiche im Mittelalter," *Germania*, IX (1864), 385–402.